D0635977

RURAL YOUTH TODAY

I. M. Slepenkov B.V. Knyazev

Introduction and translation by

James Riordan
University of Bradford, England.

ORIENTAL RESEARCH PARTNERS
Newtonville, Mass.
1977

ISBN 0-89250-009-3

For a brochure describing our Russian memoir Series, Biography Series and general line of Slavic books, please write to the Editor, Dr. P. Clendenning,
Oriental Research Partners, Box 158, Newtonville, Mass. 02168. USA.

CONTENTS

Introductory Note by James Riordan

A Note on Translation

Russian Edition Introduction

I ... Rural Youth as an Object of Sociological Research 6

II .. Working and Living Conditions of Soviet Rural Youth 27

III.. Socially-Useful Work as a Social Orientation 44

IV .. Social and Political Activity 60

V .. Moral Outlook of Rural Youth 70

VI .. Leisure Activities 86

Conclusions 104

Notes 106

Bibliography 111

Introductory Note

It is the firm belief of many writers, Western and Soviet, that the Russian peasant should be the starting point of any profound study of Soviet Society. It is, after all, within the lifetime of the present Soviet leaders that the USSR was an 80-per-cent peasant, largely illiterate land; their grandparents were probably serfs — a socio-economic status that died out in Britain some two hundred years *before it developed* in Russia. If that comparative perspective illumines the recent rural backwardness of Russia, it is even more startling to recall that in the space of fifty years, 1926 – 1976, the rural-urban population balance in European Russia has shifted dramatically from 80 : 20 to 40 : 60 – a rate of change unparallelled in history. As a Soviet demographer has recently observed, "the countryside has moved to the town." [1] This is true for European Russia, but the rural exodus is certainly far less pronounced in more traditional family orientated ethnic areas of the country as the following table shows:

RURAL POPULATION AS A PERCENT OF TOTAL POPULATION AND TOTAL NATIONALITY, BY REPUBLIC AND BY NATIONALITY: 1959 AND 1970

Republic	Total republic population 1959 (1)	Total republic population 1970 (2)	Nationality population 1959 (3)	Nationality population 1970 (4)	Nationality within titular republic 1959 (5)	Nationality within titular republic 1970 (6)	Nationality
U.S.S.R.	52.1	43.7	52.1	43.7	[1]	[1]	
Baltic republics	51.7	42.6	58.7	49.9	59.7	50.8	Baltic nationalities:
Estonia	43.5	35.0	52.9	44.9	53.1	45.3	Estonians.
Latvia	43.9	37.5	52.5	47.3	53.3	48.3	Latvians.
Lithuania	61.4	49.8	64.9	53.3	66.4	54.1	Lithuanians.
R.S.F.S.R.	47.6	37.7	42.3	32.0	45.1	34.4	Russians.
Belorussia	69.2	56.6	67.6	56.3	74.5	62.9	Belorussians.
Ukraine	54.3	45.5	60.8	51.5	63.4	54.2	Ukrainians.
Moldavia	77.7	68.3	87.1	79.6	90.4	82.8	Moldavians.
Transcaucasian republics	54.1	48.9	57.6	51.1	60.5	53.0	Transcaucasians:
Georgia	57.6	52.2	63.9	56.0	65.1	57.2	Georgians.
Armenia	50.0	40.5	43.4	35.2	47.8	37.3	Armenians.
Azerbaydzhan	52.2	49.9	65.2	60.3	63.7	58.7	Azerbaydzhani.
Kazakhstan	56.2	49.7	75.9	73.3	75.7	73.7	Kazakhs.
Central Asia	65.1	61.9	79.1	75.3	80.2	76.5	Central Asians:
Uzbekistan	66.4	63.4	78.2	75.1	79.8	77.0	Uzbeks.
Turkmenia	53.8	52.1	74.6	69.0	73.7	68.3	Turkmen.
Kirgiziya	66.3	62.6	89.2	85.4	89.0	85.5	Kirgiz.
Tadzhikistan	67.4	62.9	79.4	74.0	80.4	74.5	Tadzhiks.

[1] Not applicable.

SOURCE

Cols. 1 and 2: TsSU SSSR, "Narodnoye khozyaystvo SSSR v 1974 godu; statisticheskiy yeghegodnik," Moscow, Statistika, 1975, pp. 9–11.

Col. 3: TsSU SSSR, "Itogi Vsesoyuznoy perepisi naseleniya 1959 goda SSSR (svodnyy tom)," Moscow, Statistika, 1962, pp. 184 and 196.

Col. 4: TsSU SSSR, "Itogi Vsesoyuznoy perepisi naseleniya 1970 goda; national'nyy sostav naseleniya SSSR, soyuznykh i avtonomnykh respublik, krayev, oblastey i natsional'nykh okrugov, vol. IV, Moscow, Statistika, 1973, pp. 20 and 35.

Col. 5: Table 53 in the corresponding census volume for each republic of the 1959 census.

Col. 6: TsSU SSSR, "Itogi," vol. IV, 1973, pp. 43, 55, 152, 164, 192, 195, 202, 208, 223, 229, 253, 256, 263, 267, 273, 275, 276, 278, 280, 282, 284, 288, 295, 297, 303, 305, 306, 309, 317, and 319.

One corollary of this rural-urban continuum is that today most townsmen are still only first or second generation urbanites. Just as relevant to an understanding of contemporary Soviet rural life is the massive upheaval that has taken place over the last sixty years: of revolutions, civil war, intervention and famine, collectivisation and two devastating world wars, the second of which removed most able-bodied men from the land, never to return. It would, indeed, be remarkable if these cataclysmic events had left the peasant unscathed; whether they have transformed the old peasant culture into a new (socialist) quality remains to be proven. The value of the present investigation into rural life, however, is that it studies the ways in which the young agricultural population has discarded features normally characteristic of peasant cultures. The study is important not only because it sheds light on a hitherto 'dark' area of Soviet life; more significantly in the international perspective, it provides evidence of rural change that may, in the long run, be of greater relevance to today's predominantly agricultural nations of the Third World than that of the industrial West.

Structure of Soviet Agriculture

Soviet agriculture contains production units unknown to farming in the West — the state farm or *sovkhoz,* and the collective farm or *kolkhoz.*

State farms were set up after the Revolution, often on the basis of sequestered estates, to supply the towns and army with food, to exploit the advantages of large-scale production and to pioneer a form of socialist farming. They are run by managers appointed by the Ministry of Agriculture and employ workers who enjoy a similar status to industrial workers — i.e., they receive a monthly wage and bonuses, holidays with pay and State welfare benefits. All agricultural labourers on a sovkhoz are classified as workers *(rabochie),* not peasants *(krestyanye)*.

Collective farms existed in a few cooperative forms after the Revolution, but they proliferated after the collectivisation drive that began in 1929. The kolkhoz uses nationalised land leased in perpetuity by the State, but it owns its own implements, seeds, livestock, farm-buildings and produce. It is therefore a form of farming cooperative rather than a unit of state socialism. The kolkhoz Charter gives members the right to elect a chairman and a board which runs the farm, thus being only indirectly subordinate to the central planning authorities. The farm receives an order for produce from the government which it pays for such deliveries at fixed prices. Any surplus may be sold freely on the market. Until the late 1950's, most kolkhozniks were paid according to the *trudoden'* or labour-day system; nowadays, they are paid a monthly wage in combination with a complex system of accounting for time worked, norms fulfilled and output [2]. In addition, the farmer's family has some livestock of its own and a small allotment for private cultivation. The kolkhoznik is, therefore, a smallholder in his own right.

The most remarkable change in farming in recent years has been the trend away from kolkhozes to sovkhozes: in the twenty years up to 1970, the latter trebled in number, while the former decreased by 6.7 times[3]; kolkhozes now account for forty per cent of all cultivated land and gross farm production, less than half the marketable produce and the pastures[4]. The table below shows this trend clearly.

A Comparison of State and Collective Farms, Selected Years, 1940 – 1972

Index	1940	1950	1960	1965	1970	1972
Number of state farms	4,159	4,988	7,375	11,681	14,958	15,747
Number of collective farms	235,500	121,400	44,000	36,900	33,800	32,100
Arable land utilised by state farms (mln. ha.)	11.56	15.90	67.21	89.06	91.75	96.56
Arable land utilised by collective farms (mln. ha.)	117.72	121.00	123.02	105.07	99.05	97.62

Sources: *Narodnoye khozyaistvo SSSR, 1922 – 1972,* Moscow, 1972, p. 240; *Narodnoye khozyaistvo SSSR v 1972 g.,* Moscow, 1973, pp. 306, 313.

Although collective farms were twice as numerous as state farms in 1972, they cultivated roughly the same amount of land. State farms, were, however, much bigger – 21,000 hectares against 6,100 hectares on average[5].

Land size may be misleading in that it is the intensity of cultivation that determines yields. And in 1972, the private allotments, while accounting for just over three per cent of all arable land, contributed 1 per cent of cereals, 65 per cent of potatoes, 40 per cent of vegetables, 34 per cent of meat, 46 per cent of milk, 54 per cent of eggs and 19 per cent of wool[6]. This produce, together with the collective farm surplus, is sold at free-market prices on the seven thousand markets provided by the government in urban areas.

Soviet farm production is more backward than that of the USA or Great Britain. While agricultural employment in the Soviet Union is four-and-a-half times as high as the American and sown area is nearly twice as great, Soviet yields per man and per acre are well below the American; so, too, is the number of tractors and combine harvesters and the amount of fertiliser used. Thus, in 1966, the number of tractors used was 33 per cent, combine harvesters 52 per cent and fertiliser 36 per cent per pound per acre of the respective American figures[7]. It has been estimated that for every worker in American agriculture there was, in 1972, the equivalent of 125 hectares of cultivated land, whereas the comparable Soviet figure was nine hectares[8]. Climatic conditions partly account for this difference: thus, some ninety per cent of American and only thirty five per cent of Soviet land has favourable climatic conditions for farming; sixty per cent of arable land in the USA has an annual rainfall of 700 mm or more by contrast to only 1.1 per cent of Soviet arable land[9]. One can, however, take this too far given the fact that Canada's very large agricultural output is grown in latitudes comparable to that of the USSR.

Table 2. ANNUAL AVERAGE EMPLOYMENT IN THE STATE SECTOR, BY BRANCH OF THE ECONOMY, U.S.S.R.: 1950–75

[In thousands; figures in parentheses were interpolated linearly]

Year	Total	Agri-culture	Nonagricultural branches														
			Total	Indus-try	Con-struc-tion	For-estry	Trans-port	Com-muni-cations	Trade, public dining mate-rial-technical supply and sales, and procurement	Housing communal economy and personal services	Health services	Educa-tion and culture	Art	Science and sci-entific services	Credit and insurance organi-zations	Govern-ment adminis-tration	Other
1950	40,420	3,437	36,983	15,317	3,278	444	4,117	542	3,360	1,371	2,051	3,315	185	714	264	1,831	194
1951	[1] 42,300	(3,565)	38,735	16,230	3,414	(453)	(4,370)	(554)	(3,444)	(1,428)	(2,139)	(3,434)	(194)	(772)	(263)	(1,809)	231
1952	[1] 43,900	3,693	40,207	16,873	3,578	462	4,623	565	3,528	1,485	2,226	3,553	(202)	829	262	1,786	235
1953	[1] 45,400	4,026	41,374	17,617	3,685	416	4,694	582	3,496	1,519	2,308	3,647	(211)	860	263	1,726	250
1954	[1] 49,100	5,966	43,134	18,499	4,064	(402)	(4,925)	(596)	(3,626)	(1,551)	(2,468)	(3,817)	(219)	(926)	(264)	(1,544)	233
1955	50,251	6,041	44,210	18,984	4,119	389	5,056	611	3,756	1,583	2,627	3,988	288	992	265	1,361	251
1956	51,869	5,954	45,915	19,702	4,523	390	5,232	624	3,826	1,666	2,736	4,103	(245)	1,094	266	1,342	166
1957	54,460	6,628	47,832	20,357	5,014	377	5,368	641	4,017	1,721	2,892	4,250	(263)	1,208	261	1,294	169
1958	56,005	6,005	50,000	20,997	5,495	367	5,681	664	4,190	1,754	3,059	4,378	(280)	1,338	260	1,294	243
1959	57,867	5,568	52,299	21,670	5,921	352	5,984	691	4,389	1,815	3,245	4,556	(298)	1,474	260	1,273	371
1960	62,032	6,793	55,239	22,620	6,319	359	6,279	738	4,675	1,920	3,461	4,803	315	1,763	265	1,245	477
1961	65,861	7,496	58,365	23,817	6,541	378	6,518	790	5,010	2,030	3,677	5,165	346	2,011	277	1,295	510
1962	68,300	7,817	60,483	24,677	6,523	389	6,677	832	5,253	2,096	3,818	5,521	340	2,213	283	1,316	545
1963	70,526	7,954	62,572	25,442	6,684	399	6,841	877	5,487	2,182	3,933	5,835	353	2,370	289	1,308	572
1964	73,258	8,168	65,090	26,317	6,883	404	7,054	928	5,752	2,282	4,082	6,204	362	2,497	296	1,354	675
1965	76,915	8,704	68,211	27,447	7,301	402	7,252	1,007	6,009	2,386	4,277	6,600	370	2,625	300	1,460	775
1966	79,709	8,894	70,815	28,514	7,549	409	7,364	1,073	6,261	2,489	4,427	6,895	380	2,741	313	1,546	854
1967	82,274	8,836	73,438	29,448	7,880	412	7,467	1,123	6,575	2,674	4,545	7,172	387	2,850	329	1,651	925
1968	85,100	8,899	76,201	30,428	8,149	421	7,606	1,187	6,964	2,800	4,747	7,507	393	2,990	346	1,736	927
1969	87,922	9,083	78,839	31,159	8,572	426	7,803	1,269	7,287	2,930	4,927	7,777	403	3,128	363	1,834	961
1970	90,186	9,180	81,006	31,593	9,052	433	7,985	1,330	7,537	3,052	5,080	8,025	412	3,238	388	1,883	998
1971	92,799	9,499	83,300	32,030	9,549	432	8,203	1,394	7,816	3,213	5,239	8,262	420	3,374	411	1,935	1,022
1972	95,242	9,647	85,595	32,461	9,986	443	8,446	1,435	8,100	3,376	5,386	8,482	428	3,544	439	2,008	1,061
1973	97,466	9,885	87,581	32,875	10,091	444	8,705	1,465	8,392	3,527	5,522	8,708	434	3,735	465	2,087	1,131
1974	99,780	10,102	89,678	33,433	10,339	449	8,922	1,499	8,640	3,664	5,655	8,924	441	3,864	493	2,168	1,187
1975	102,155	10,330	91,825	34,030	10,550	450	9,150	1,540	8,890	3,815	5,790	9,145	445	4,010	520	2,240	1,250

[1] Data were reported as rounded to tenths of millions.

Source: Stephen Rapawy, "Estimates and Projections of the Labor Force and Civilian Employment in the U.S.S.R.: 1950 to 1990," U.S. Department of Commerce, Bureau of Economic Analysis, 1976 (forthcoming).

Soviet Rural Sociology

Interest in rural sociology in Russia goes back to before the Revolution. Shortly after the first Russian Census of 1897, a detailed census of the rural population was carried out by several provincial health departments; they produced detailed statistics on cultural and living standards, housing, employment, vital indices, age structure, educational standards and property-ownership[10]. After 1917, similar statistics-gathering studies were undertaken. In 1923, a large-scale study of 3,000 households was made in seven provinces and, in 1924-25, some 33,000 households were examined[11]. An empirical study of the Bol'shevereisk District in Voronezh Province in 1925 produced an interesting insight into living conditions: half the peasants slept on top of their stoves and only three per cent (mostly kulaks) in beds; sixty per cent of the peasants thought it necessary to beat their wives – for educational purposes; eighty per cent of the peasants stated that they could not do without State-produced vodka 'as a stimulant and a medicine'; eighty-five per cent of the homes were infested with cockroaches, fleas or bed-bugs; the wealthier peasants gave a smaller proportion of their income to the Church than the poorer peasants, etc.[12].

Much of the research of the 1920's, and even more so in the years to come, was sponsored by the Party for purely practical ends, to provide solutions to practical problems, mostly basic questions of Party policy. Nonetheless, despite the methodological weaknesses and lack of trained sociologists, the research provides a valuable picture of the period and a source of comparison with later years. From the end of the 1920's until the Twentieth Party Congress in 1956, rural sociology – like Soviet sociology in general – became dormant or was confined to descriptive, rather idealised studies. One of the major reasons for the rejuvenation of rural sociology after Stalin's death was the reform programme of Party Secretary N.S. Khrushchov, who moved the peasant to the forefront of Soviet politics, thereby setting in motion a relatively frank debate about the Soviet countryside – quite at variance with the earlier ritualistic evocations of a flourishing collective farming. Although many rural studies still contain a number of acknowledged shortcomings – uncertain methodology, avoidance of 'awkward' areas and questions[13], an elliptic style that presents an introduction and conclusions incongruosly (and often deliberately) at odds with the research findings, and the irritating disease of 'quotationitis' – they are increasingly producing much frank and perceptive information about the Soviet countryside.

Slepenkov and Knyazev base their study on nearly seventy villages in eighteen regions of the country. In a land as large and diverse as the USSR, such a representative survey ranging from the Ukraine to Siberia, from Latvia to Tadzhikistan, is likely to avoid the parochialness of single-area studies. The books present material on the attitudes of rural youth to farm work, village life, private plots, earnings, leisure, the town and many other problems; it also provides a revealing insight into the living and working conditions of young farmers. Rural attitudes and conditions make interesting comparisons with those of urban workers portrayed in recent Soviet urban sociology, such as I.P. Trufanov's *Problems of Soviet Urban Life*[14]. In view of the declared Soviet intention of bringing the gap between urban and rural life as a prerequisite of complete communist society, it is worth comparing such indices as job-satisfaction, free-time expenditure, family-size and attitudes, household furnishings and equipment in town and country. The indications in the present book are that a number of factors, including the socialist organisation of work, education, modern technology, the mass media and communist socialisation, are important vehicles of cultural change, especially among young people, in replacing a deeply-rooted 'peasant outlook' by one more appropriate to a modern complex industrial society. There seems evidence that a 'socialist consciousness', as distinct from a modern consumerism, is also developing among young people on the basis of their experience of life and work within the collective. In these respects, the essential differences between town and country seem to be fading. But intractable problems remain, as the book alludes to, which are partly responsible for the 'flight from the land', mainly of young people, at the current rate of nearly two million every year [15].

The book does not, however, deal with the enormous inequalities that have confronted the rural dweller over the years: the need to carry an "internal passport" which was required until 1975 for movement about the country, the many prohibitions preventing him from settling in large cities and the low rate of acceptance of rural youth in good universities and technical schools in the most favoured cities. Nor does the book adequately treat the whole problem of the "private plot"; it is not, dramatically decreasing every year as have been shown in a recent study by Murray Feshbach and Stephen Rapawy [16].

Lastly, of course, there is no direct reference to the continued inability of Soviet agricultural output to meet the domestic demand. The recent (1975-76) Soviet purchase of Canadian and American grain attest to the chronic under-capitalisation and mis-management of Soviet agriculture; the reader should be warned that the omission of these facts reflects current Soviet thinking and statistics and convey several levels of truth and falsehood. Nevertheless, it is to the credit of the authors that many problems are dealt with openly, thus enhancing our understanding of life and labour in the modern Soviet village.

Notes

1 V. Perevedentsev, *Nash sovremennik,* No. 11, 1972, p. 100.

2 For an authoritative account of remuneration, see K. —E. Wädekin, *Die Bezahlung der Arbeit in der sowjetischen Landwirtschaft,* Berlin (West), 1972. See, too, K. —E. Wädekin, "Income Distribution in Soviet Agriculture", *Soviet Studies,* Jan., 1975, No. 1, pp. 3 – 26.

3 S.I. Semin, *Preodelenie sotsial 'no-ekonomicheskikh razlichiy mezhdu gorodom i derevnei,* Moscow, 1973, p. 111.

4 *Ibid.,* p. 43.

5 *SSSR v tsifrakh v 1972 godu,* Moscow, 1973, pp. 136, 139.

6 *Ibid.,* p. 106.

7 See H.E. Walters, "Agriculture in the United States and USSR", *New Directions in the Soviet Economy,* Washington, 1966, p. 478.

U.S.S.R. AND UNITED STATES: AGRICULTURAL PROFILE, 1974

	U.S.S.R.	United States	U.S.S.R. as a percent of United States
Agriculture's share of gross national product (percent)[1]	17.6	2.6	NA
Agriculture's share of the labor force (percent)	26.3	3.7	NA
New fixed investment in agriculture per worker as a percent of new fixed investment per worker in industry (percent)	.5	3.2	NA
Area sown (million hectares)	216.5	[2] 137.4	157.6
Fertilizer application (million metric tons of nutrients)	15.0	[3] 17.5	85.7
Stock of agricultural machinery (thousands):			
Tractors	2,267	4,376	51.8
Trucks	1,336	2,906	45.9
Combines	673	698	96.4
Agricultural output:			
Food grain:[4]			
Area (million hectares)	70.0	20.5	341.5
Production (million metric tons)	[5] 89.9	43.5	206.7
Yield (centners per hectare)	12.8	21.3	60.1
Feed grain:[6]			
Area (million hectares)	46.6	35.1	132.8
Production (million metric tons)	[5] 72.6	133.9	54.2
Yield (centners per hectare)	15.6	38.1	40.9
Potatoes (million metric tons)	81.0	48.6	166.7
Meat (million metric tons)[7]	14.6	17.2	84.9
Milk (million metric tons)	91.8	[8] 52.3	175.5

1 Share of GNP at factor cost originating in agriculture in 1970 prices for the U.S.S.R. and in 1972 prices for the United States.
2 Based on 1969 land census.
3 1973.
4 Wheat, rye, and rice.
5 Official Soviet production data minus an estimated 3 percent handling loss and an estimated 8 percent waste resulting from excess moisture and extraneous matter. See footnote 2 on p. 576.
6 Corn, oats, and barley.
7 Carcass weight equivalent. U.S. data exclude edible byproducts (horsemeat, rabbit, poultry game, edible offal, and lard).
8 Whole milk.

Source: Data are in large part found in "Survey of Current Business" and "Agricultural Statistics: 1975" for the United States, "Narodnoye khozyaystvo S.S.S.R. v 1974 godu" for the U.S.S.R. Methodology for computing GNP data for the U.S.S.R. is discussed in "U.S.S.R.: Gross National Product Accounts, 1970," Central Intelligence Agency, A(ER) 75-76, November 1975.

8 I.H. Hill, 'The End of the Russian Peasantry", *Soviet Studies,* Jan., 1975, No. 1, p. 114.

9 V.I. Staroverov, *Gorod ili derevnya,* Moscow, 1972, p. 84.

10 A.I. Shingarev, *Umirayushaya derevnya,* 2nd edn. Petrograd, 1907; S.V. Martynov, *Sovremennye usloviya v Russkoi derevne,* Saratov, 1903.

11 *Raionnye ispolnitel'nye komitety i sel'skie sovety,* Moscow, 1924; Ya. Shafir, *Pechat' i derevnya,* Moscow-Leningrad, 1924.

12 F. Zheleznev, *Voronezhskaya derevnya,* Pervy vypusk, Bol'shevereisky raion, Voronezh, 1926. For further details of the development of Soviet rural sociology, see Yu.V. Arutyunyan, *Opyt sotsiologicheskovo izucheniya sela,* Moscow, 1968.

13 In the present monograph, for example, Table 29 contains answers to questions concerning the maintenance, reduction and abolition of private allotments. Yet there is no question on whether farmers wish to increase the size of private allotments!

14 I.P. Trufanov, *Problems of Soviet Urban Life,* published in English by Oriental Research Partners in 1976.

15 *Zhurnalist,* 1973, No. 1, p. 36.

16 See TsSU's discussion in *Narodnoye Khozyai'stuo SSSR v 1974 godu, statisticheskii ezhegodnik.* (Moscow, 1975), pp. 832-3.

17 Murray Feshbach, Stephen Rapawy, "Population and Manpower Trends and Policies". An essay to be published in U.S. Congress, Joint Economic Committee, SOVIET ECONOMY IN A NEW PERSPECTIVE 1976 (forthcoming).

James Riordan,
University of Bradford,
1976.

SELECT FURTHER READINGS

1 J.R. Millar, *The Soviet Rural Community,* Urbana, Ill. 1971.

2 Karl-Eugen Wädekin, *Privat-produzentin in der sowjetischen Landwirtschaft.* Koln, 1969.

3 NATO, Economic Directorate, (ed) *Symposium, 14 – 16 April, 1971,* "Soviet Economic Growth", rev. ed, Brussels, 1975.

4 *Ibid, Colloquium, 29 – 31 January, 1975,* "Economic Aspects of Life in the USSR". Brussels, 1975. A splendid series of valuable essays.

A Note On Translation

In translating terms for which no ready English equivalents exist I have, as a rule, used the nearest English equivalent. Sometimes, however, I have had to use an invented term that is in common use among students of Soviet society. I give a list of the most common below. While maintaining the sense and accuracy of the original, I have taken the liberty of making amendments to the text to improve readability. I have checked quotations of foreign authors with the originals wherever possible and written foreign names in full where Western usage makes this desirable. Similarly, I have tidied up footnotes and tables according to Western practice -- adding, for example, numbers and headings for all tables. I have also added my own explanatory footnotes as a guide for the reader. Transliteration of Russian technical terms has been kept as consistent as possible throughout.

Glossary of common non-equivalent terms

akkordno-premial'naya sistema - piecework-and-bonus system
byt- everyday life
domashyny inventar' - household inventory: furniture and domestic equipment
dosug- leisure
dolzhnost' - job-responsibility
GTO (*Gotov k trudu i oborone*)- "Ready for Labour and Defence"/ national fitness programme
ITR (*inzhenerno-tekhnicheskie rabotniki*) - engineering and technical personnel
kolkhoz - collective farm

Komsomol - Young Communist League
krai - territory
kul'turno-bytovoi fond - cultural-and-everyday-needs fund
mekhanizator - machine-operator
oblast' - region

obshchestvennaya rabota - social work

obshchestvennye fondy - public consumption funds

peredovik - front-line worker

podsobnoye khozyaistvo - home farm

polevod - field worker

rabochiy - industrial manual worker

raion - district

sadovo-ogorodny uchastok - garden allotment and orchard

sadovoi uchastok - garden allotment

sel'sovet - village Soviet (council)

sluzhashchiy - employee

sovkhoz - state farm

subbotnik - voluntary unpaid work on a Saturday

trudoden' - labour-day (payment)

voskresnik - voluntary unpaid work on a Sunday

zhivotnovod - stockman

zveno - 'link-system'

Editor's Note: As of April, 1976, the Soviet Government stated the rouble (100 kopecks) was officially worth $1.30; the "unofficial" rate (black market) was approximately 3 roubles per dollar.

Introduction

Fresh generations of young people are constantly being drawn into the revolutionary process of social regeneration of the contemporary world. Every society and its classes are concerned with the way young people act and think; they endeavour to mould a certain type of personality, to instill in it traits and qualities that ensure a level and direction of activity which involve young people in resolving the complex problems of our day. What sort of people are they that make up the younger generation? What are their aims and attitudes to life? These are questions that are acquiring increasing social significance.

Young people in Soviet society have immense scope for manifesting creative endeavour and talent in transforming every facet of life. The creative part they play and their vital place in building socialism and communism are bound up with the concern of the Party and the entire nation for the education of the younger generation -- capable of "worthily continuing the cause of their fathers, the cause of the great Lenin". As L.I. Brezhnev said in his report "Fifty Years of Great Socialist Victories", "Socialism is a society without privileged classes or estates; but one section of the population gained privilege from the very first days of Soviet Power: that is our children, our young people."[1]

Soviet youth are in the front ranks of the army of builders of communism; they uphold and develop the traditions of the older generation. They are selflessly working at factories and mills, collective and state farms, mastering science and technology; they are gaining wide-ranging opportunities to take an energetic part in all spheres of social life. "The working class, collective-farm peasants and the Soviet intelligentsia," note the Documents of the 24th Party Congress, "are being replenished by cultured and specialist personnel capable of tackling any complex problem that may arise during the scientific and technological revolution."[2]

The Congress decisions are permeated with deep concern and solicitude for the harmonious development of the younger generation, the further enhancement of the social role of all sections of young people in the life of Soviet society. "The widest possible horizons are opening up for young people to apply their enthusiasm, energy and knowledge."[3]

The Party calls upon young people "to be in the front line of the struggle to create a new and sophisticated technology, to employ it consistently in all branches of the economy and to raise the productivity and culture of labour, to affirm in everyday life new and truly communist social relationships and the lofty principles of communist morality"[4]. The participation of young people in implementing the Party resolutions is currently a characteristic feature of their training for and involvement in an independent life and the basic social mechanism. The Leninist Komsomol is tackling the difficult task of transforming the creative endeavour of young people into a might school of communist education and of shaping the personality of the young Soviet worker.

In enhancing the part played by youth in the struggle for communism, the Party regards it of the utmost importance to take careful consideration of social change and concrete conditions, to study the interests and requirements of young people. In such circumstances, it is appropriate to make a theoretical study of the problems of youth, their life and labour, education and recreation among various groups of Soviet young people. Such groups of industrial workers, farmers, specialists, students and schoolchildren all possess their own characteristics, the study and significance of which are necessary for sensible leadership and effective educative work with each of them[5].

This book contains the results of concrete sociological research among young people in the Soviet countryside today. The surveys were carried out between 1967 and 1971 by the Rural Youth Section of the Central Committee of the All-Union Leninist Communist Youth League and the Sociological Research Laboratory of the Scientific Commission Department of the M.V. Lomonosov Moscow State University Philosophy Faculty.

In the course of our research, we carried out a wide-ranging programme of studies into social aspects of the rural way of life of young people, their ideals and aspirations, requirements and interests, their role in social and economic change and in raising the cultural standards of the Soviet village.

In so far as rural studies include such a wide range of economic, social, psychological and ideological problems, we focused attention largely on the following:

What are the specific characteristics of Soviet rural youth?

In what ways are the status and orientation of different groups of rural youth changing in line with the socio-economic transformation of village life, the rapid growth of forces of production and the impact of science and technology on farming?

What differences are there in the social behaviour and outlook of rural youth in relation to their branch of production, organisation of labour and the collective, and the cultural development of the village?

Are there any appreciable differences in the status and orientation of rural youth in regard to sex, education and occupation?

In what way do they take part in labour and socio-political life, what are their spiritual and cultural requirements and what opportunities exist for meeting them?

By studying these questions, we can sketch a social portrait of contemporary rural youth; we can establish the relationships and interaction between the specific conditions and the life-plans and social behaviour of young people in the village as they enter upon their independent worklife.

We hope that this work, being an attempt at a comprehensive rural youth study, will make its modest contribution to the communist socialisation of the younger generation and will help the Leninist _Komsomol_ to guide Soviet rural youth.

Research Methods. In elaborating our research methods, we primarily took into consideration the need to provide an all-round picture of rural youth as a socio-demographic group in society. Our aim was to give our subject flesh and blood by analysis of statistics, supplementary data, concrete methods and empirical sociological research. Our main research methods were to conduct questionnaires and to collect information about rural youth by sample surveys.

The two following features characterise our chosen sample method:

(i) selection of locations where we could conduct the investigation according to our overall programme;

(ii) selection of groups of people (units of the sample total) at the chosen locations which constituted the sample total.

1. Selection of locations was a fairly complicated business, inasmuch as we had to choose places whose study would enable us to make generalisations about the research subject. In our zonal sample scheme we included several regions of the country in which we defined rural districts, village councils and work-groups directly for the study of our sociological expeditions. The regions and republics we chose were as follows: the Kostroma, Kalinin, Ryazan, Saratov, Voronezh, Kurgan, Irkutsk and Amur regions, the Krasnodar Territory, the Mari Autonomous Soviet Socialist Republic, the Ukraine (Zhitomir Region), Armenia, Tadzhikistan and Latvia. In selecting the districts and villages, we were governed by various criteria in relation to the set programme.

We concentrated mainly on economic geography and demography, the economic profile and level of development, extent of remoteness from industrial centres, etc. One or two rural districts were included in the survey within each region (territory or republic).

In selecting villages, we took the following into consideration:

a) districts with a predominant form of production-organisation(collective or state farm);

b) collective or state farms at different economic levels;

c) collective and state farms of different types and specialisation, according to economic indicators;

d) types of settlement and number of villagers (up to 100, 300, 600, 1000 households, over 1000 households);

e) the factor of territorial remoteness from the town and highway communications -- we selected villages situated within 10 kilometres from the town, from 15 to 30-50 kilometres; over 50 kilometres; those located far from the main thoroughfares, regional and district centres.

In accordance with our programme sample, we studied a total of 68 villages and 18 rural districts in the above-mentioned regions and republics.

11. We had to ensure that all youth groups were represented in our sample. Further, the proportions of different groups of employed rural youth within the sample had to correspond to the objective structure of rural youth

in the country as a whole. We fixed the age perimetres of young people in our sample at 15 and 30.

The sampling procedure normally took place as follows:

1. On the basis of registration books, we compiled a list of all young people in the village between 15 and 30 with an indication of sex, age and occupation.

2. We selected people for the survey from the list depending on payment rates; this selection was made mechanically, at certain intervals.

3. We tested the sample by adjusting the group representation by type of job, sex, age and pre-selection of people with certain trades (for example, agronomists, livestock specialists, mechanical engineers -- people who comprised the smallest proportion of all groups of employed rural youth).

On the whole, the selection procedure ensured that every unit of the total had an equal chance of being selected.

The dimensions of the sample were determined as follows:

--50 per cent of young people in villages up to 300 households;
30 per cent in villages up to 600 households;
20 per cent in villages up to 1000 households;
15 per cent in villages over 1000 households.

During the actual sampling we made certain deviations from these standards for various reasons. Nonetheless, these deviations occurred only with an insignificant number of units. As a result, 4,200 people or 15 per cent of the total were included in the survey out of an aggregate of 28,100 young farmers from the villages under study. Further, 1,800 schoolchildren in the eighth to tenth classes of village schools filled in questionnaires.

The following methods of research were employed:

1. A question-form for each village was filled in for each village chosen for a sociological survey of working youth and schoolchildren. The form was designed for collecting objective data and information typifying the economic life of rural labour teams, the composition of the population, cultural standards, everyday life and the activity of public organisations.

2. Interview-questionnaires for asking questions of working youth.

3. A questionnaire for village school-leavers.

4. An interview-questionnaire for the 'intelligentsia' -- those who had worked more than ten years in the countryside.

5. An interview-questionnaire for older people in the village.

6. Instructions on the procedure for gathering objective data and for using questionnaires.

The research programme was drawn up by staff at the Sociological Research Laboratory of the Scientific Atheism Department at the M.V. Lomonosov Moscow State University Philosophy Faculty, headed by I.M. Slepenkov.

The following laboratory members took part in gathering and processing data: S.Ye. Alexandrova, A.I. Demodova, V.A. Provotorov, A.I. Yefimova, V.B. Kulakov, Yu.I. Delyagin, V.I. Dmitriev and V.N. Mikhailov.

Computer processing of the programme and sociological information was carried out by E.A. Abgaryan, Candidate of Philosophical Sciences.

The authors would like to express their deep gratitude to B.A. Shuvalov, Candidate of Philosophical Sciences and co-author of Chapter 4, and to Professor Yu.V. Arutyunyan, V.T. Duvakin, Yu.V. Torsuev and V.S. Yaroshovts who provided much assistance in preparing and carrying out the research.

CHAPTER ONE

RURAL YOUTH AS AN OBJECT OF SOCIOLOGICAL RESEARCH

1. Youth as a socio-demographic group in society

In studying the younger generation and defining its place and role in the life of society, we must first and foremost take a Marxist-Leninist approach; this regards youth an an integral part of society, connected with certain classes and their parties. This approach requires us to examine the question in a specific historical perspective, defining the place of young people in the social structure, explaining their role in the class struggle and their attitude to ideology and class politics.

In his comprehensive study of the position of classes and groups in society, V.I. Lenin pointed to the indissoluble link between their requirements and interests, feelings and moods, on the one hand, and the socio-economic conditions of life on the other. He was ever scornful of those who tried to explain the political aspirations of youth as "a force of ideal aspirations" among young people, rather than "the real conditions of social life in Russia". In his work "The Tasks of Revolutionary Youth", Lenin talks of student participation in the revolutionary movement, underlining that "students would not be what they were if their political grouping did not correspond to the political grouping throughout society -- 'correspond' not in the sense of direct representation of students and social groups according to their power and size, but in the sense of the necessary and inevitable presence among students of those groups that exist in society"[1].

Marxists believe that actual adherence to a social group and awareness of this adherence normally have a considerable influence on a person's destiny, his attitude to social problems. At the same time, Lenin showed that a young person's outlook is not determined automatically by his belonging to a particular class. It is shaped under the impact of the sum total of factors in social life, as a result of his active participation in the political life of society.

In the present epoch -- that of open contention between the two worlds, socialism and capitalism -- the younger generation takes shape and enters social life under the impact of two countervailing tendencies: the proletarian-socialist and the bourgeois way of life, each with their own moral standards and philosophical principles. The ruling classes of the contemporary capitalist world use the entire arsenal of economic, political and ideological weapons to keep young people within the orbit of the bourgeois way of life, its standards and principles.

In day-to-day activity and, above all, in the course of the class struggle, however, the proletariat creates its own mode of social life, the standards and principles which express the fundamental requirements and interests of the working class and of all working people, which reflect the major trends of social progress.

The ideals elaborated in the struggle and vital activity of the working class are becoming, as mentioned at the 24th Party Congress, an attractive force for all honest, progressive people of our time. The best representatives of social groups and classes are coming over to the side of the working class and socialism.

In their approach to young people, Marx, Engels and Lenin always accorded great importance to the socio-psychological, psychological and physiological characteristics associated with age, with that period in a person's life when he is getting ready to embark upon independent life. They frequently noted that young people possess attributes such as youthful romanticism and maximalism, heightened emotions, energy, an acute penchant for all that is new. Youth is part of society that has always to master a requisite 'sum of knowledge', practical experience and standards of moral conduct in order to play a successful part in socially-useful activity[2]. In the course of its socialisation, it undertakes an immense amount of work in mastering the whole system of social values.

Since the effective participation of young people in the life of society is largely associated with their involvement in independent life, it is invariably accompanied, too, by the seeking of vital orientations and insufficient stability of such orientations, subordination to various influences.

The fact that the younger generation joins in the life of society as an active force gives it an aspiration for social independence, but not for detachment -- as bourgeois ideologists try to show.

Marxists consider the independence youth to be a necessary condition of its active participation in the revolutionary transformation of the contemporary world. "Without complete independence," wrote Lenin, "young people cannot either make good socialists or prepare to take socialism forward."[3]

This independence is not an independence of a "political grouping" -- i.e., a certain class independence. On the contrary, youth's position in society, its socio-demographic characteristics demand constant attention and guidance from the older generation. Youth, at a time of the active formation of the human personality, is in particular need of guidance from a class and its political party. Only under the guidance of Marxist-Leninist parties is contemporary progressive youth capable of realising the requirements of social progress and ensuring for itself a really revolutionary, really creative participation in attaining the ideals of socialism.

A scientific approach to defining youth as a specific group in society presupposes account for more than the demographic and age characteristics of the younger generation; we must also consider the social characteristics which it acquires during its participation in all spheres of social life. It is these social characteristics that determine the direction of the social activity of different groups of young people in class society. To define youth merely as an age and demographic group means essentially glossing over the vital importance of the social class factors in the shaping of young people and in ensuring them a corresponding role in the life of society.

Youth, consequently, is a socio-demographic group in society which is characterised, on the one hand, by age and psycho-physiological attributes, by the carrying out primarily of activity connected with preparation for and inclusion in independent social life; on the other, it is distinguished by a social differentiation appropriate to the class division of society.

This Marxist-Leninist understanding of youth and its role in the life of society is opposed by a united front of bourgeois ideologists, opportunists, right- and left-wing revisionists.

Bourgeois sociologists make an absolute of the age characteristics of young people, portraying them as a special group for which age rather than class distinctions is of prime importance; they try to subordinate the younger generation to bourgeois ideology and drag it into the stream of reactionary politics. It is noteworthy that these pseudo-scientific principles often lie behind the most diverse, sometimes directly contradictory, conceptions of young people.

Within the mass of bourgeois theories about modern youth, one strand stands out in bold relief -- the idea that "class peace" and the age of affluence are arriving, that modern youth needs comfort not barricades. Thus, the West German sociologist and Social Research Laboratory chief, Helmut Schelsky, writes that it is senseless to counterpose bourgeois and working class youth, because differences in opinion among the social strata of young people have been eroded and young people, as a *transitional age group* (our italics), are adapting to the demands of the uniform contemporary industrial (i.e., 'bourgeois') society and becoming part of its 'common' organism. Youth is evidently no longer bound by the great bonds of class affiliation. Awareness of solidarity with the exploited has given way to a desire to satisfy personal requirements, to feather one's own nest. Hence the conclusion: today's youth of the capitalists states shares a certain neutrality, scepticism in regard to ideologies and a healthy consumer interest; therefore, the younger generation will not be influenced by revolution[4].

The heightened social and political activity and the mass youth demonstrations of recent years have dealt a mighty blow to such theories about a sceptical, indifferent and lost generation. Young people do not hanker after the 'paradise' of the consumer bourgeois society with its avaricious chasing after profits, its 'reification' of commodities and their tyranny over human beings, and its stultifying standardisation of the personality. As Charles Reich has written in his book *The Greening of America*, for the person setting out in life, there are no open roads either for his mind or for his soul -- only a long, hard exhausting road into nowhere[5]. *Newsweek* writes with some anguish that the ordinary American workman, particularly the young, is simply unhappy and discontent with work and life[6]. Young people are increasingly becoming aware of the falseness and decadence of the capitalist world; their discontent is breaking through to the surface and growing into open protest.

The Washington Post sounds the alarm that two-thirds of the increment in the labour force in the 1970's are young people between 16 and 34 who are already increasingly criticising official policy, openly challenging bourgeois corporations, asking such wicked and dangerous questions as "For whom are we working?" "In whose interests are we producing commodities?" The apologists of capitalism are very concerned that young "blue collar" workers are now more quickly and unmistakenly recognising the exploitative nature of capitalist production and seeking a way out in mass struggle. Confirmation of that is the 4,900 big strikes that took place in 1971 alone -- despite Washington's draconic anti-strike measures. Young people were well to the fore among strikers against the bastions of the exploiting 'social and bureaucratic organisation'.

Bourgeois ideologists of various persuasions seek increasingly to apply in these new situations pseudo-revolutionary theories that proclaim the youth to be the main revolutionary factor in the historical development of mankind, "the third major class", "the sole revolutionary force of the present"[7]. The bourgeoisie needs this type of political disorientation of the potentially progressive, but still inexperienced youth (which sometimes has only hazy notions of Marxist Leninist revolutionary theory and the real designation of the youth movement) so as to divorce it from the working class and its vanguard -- the communist party.

All these contrived theories cannot stand up to the scientific principles of Marxism concerning the social role of young people in present day society whose correctness is convincingly demonstrated by the entire course of the revolution.

The socialist system alone ensures the effective resolution of problems of youth, its purposive involvement in the creative process. For the first time in history, issues associated with the rising generation are being tackled in a conscious and planned way. The socialist state does not simply display concern for young people; it possesses real opportunities for directing and regulating the social processes on which depends the formation of the talents and requirements of young men and women.

The new system has in practice ensured a prominent place for young people in the social transofrmation of society.

To use Lenin's words, socialist construction is the affair of innovators; it is oriented on the future by a whole complex of exciting tasks. It needs young creative forces and youthful energy. That is precisely why the communist ideal has become of immense value to young people. Direct participation in the building of socialism and communism guarantees young people a real 'forging and tempering', enables them to develop an intellectual-moral and ideological-political maturity.

L.I. Brezhnev has said "that young people under 30 make up over half the population of our country. They are our future, our replacements"[8].

The most marked traits of Soviet youth are internationalism, communist conviction, socialist optimism and a fresh attitude to labour; that constitutes the basic features of the personality of young Soviet men and women. A new type of younger generation has grown up during the Soviet years.

At all stages of socialist construction, the Communist Party has displayed particular concern for young people, inculcating in them the virtues of genuine fighters for communist ideals. Being guided by Lenin's teaching, the Party has defined the basic aims of communist education of young people at the present stage of communist construction. As stressed at the 16th Congress of the Komsomol, these include:

"(i) to prepare a generation of harmoniously developed, highly-educated people, firm and selfless fighters for the victory of communism, able to administer society and the state. To teach Komsomol members, all young men and women, creatively to master Marxist-Leninist theory, to develop in them a scientific-materialist outlook, to inculcate ideological conviction, a class approach to social events and a devotion to the cause of the Party. All our young people should know Lenin's teaching, be able to live and fight in a Leninist manner;

(ii) to socialise young people through the experience of the Communist Party, through the revolutionary, war and labour traditions of the people, tirelessly to develop in them feelings of Soviet patriotism, unshakeable fraternal friendship among the peoples of the USSR and proletarian internationalism, love for the socialist Fatherland, constant readiness, weapon in hand, to defend the gains of the Revolution;

(iii) to shape in young men and women a communist attitude to work and socialist property, a lofty responsibility for the cause of the collective and society, to see that they clearly appreciate the indissoluble link between personal ideals and the great ideals of the nation;

(iv) to bring up the younger generation in a spirit of communist morals and morality, collectivism and comradeship, an intolerance of manifestations of egotism, acquisitiveness and a private proprietory psychology, of violations of the norms of the socialist community and Soviet laws;

(v) to enhance the revolutionary watchfulness of Komsomol members and all young people, firmly to develop in them an uncompromising attitude to brougeois ideology and morality, to attempts by imperialist propaganda to turn their heads by false slogans of 'class peace', and mercilessly to expose the reactionary essence of capitalism."[9]

The work of the Leninist Komsomol and all sections of Soviet youth is now being turned to fulfil these lofty Party behests formalised in the decisions of the 24th Party Congress.

Soviet youth, being in a moral-political sense a monolithic part of society with a clearly-expressed tendency towards social heterogeneity, reflects in its make-up the class structure of our society. Moreover, youth as a socio-demographic group in its internal structure has its own distinctive features.

In studying the problems of life and labour of young people, it is important methodologically to differentiate and define the concrete object of research, to determine its place in the overall system. In this investigation, the object of study is the youth of the present-day Soviet village, which today makes up a sizeable part of Soviet young people. Virtually every fifth resident in the Soviet village is today in the 15-30 age group. The importance of a comprehensive study of rural youth comes not merely from its high proportion among rural dwellers, but above all from the social perspective -- the huge tasks of economically and culturally transforming the village.

Rural youth has traversed a glorious and, at the same time, arduous road in fighting for the establishment of the new way of life in the Soviet countryside. The best representatives of rural youth, communists and Komsomol members, have been in the front line of this struggle for the new life. They "ploughed up not only old field-boundary lines, but also old habits, the whole age-old tenor of village life"[10].

The participation of rural youth in building socialism and communism, along with all Soviet young people, along with the whole Soviet people, produced in it the same traits and qualities of advanced fighters which are inherent in the young men and women of our country. Nonetheless, the specific conditions of life and labour left their mark on all aspects of their lives. In their own way they manifest the common traits of Soviet youth, revealing them in the specific nature of their requirements and interests, their vital plans and value-orientations, which have to be taken into account. In describing rural youth as an object of sociological research, we must first elucidate its internal structure.

2. Structure of youth in the contemporary Soviet village

When we examine the social status of young people, we do not confine our Marxist approach to a single characteristic that distinguishes it as a socio-demographic group in society. This methodological tenet has particular theoretical importance in defining the structure of youth. The approach enables us to determine both the social role of young people as a whole and their individual structural formations, their specific features and the place they occupy in social life.

The social uniformity of Soviet youth, by virtue of public ownership, the moral-political unity of society and the prevalence of communist ideology, does not yet signify its complete homogeneity. The fact that it belongs to a particular class, an occupationsl group or type of settlement, and the nature of its work, all produce a whole number of levels in youth structure. Each opens up possibliities for social characterisation. It is therefore important to determine the distinguishing features which are fundamental for a particular youth structure.

If we look at the social class division of our socialist society as the basis of youth structure, then youth may be divided into the following categories:

1. young industrial workers;
2. young collective farmers;
3. young people who belong to the stratum of the intelligentsia.

Another way of classifying youth structure is to distinguish different occupations. Thus, we may classify the following groups: young people working in industry; young people working in agriculture; young people working in transport; young people working in services, etc.

Another method is to take types of human settlement. Thus:

1. urban youth;
2. rural youth.

Each youth group constitutes an integral structural formation and is distinguished, in turn, bu its internal differentiation. Each depends on the presence in socialist society of essential socio-economic and cultural differences due to the level of economic development and the division of social labour. It is therefore important to differentiate youth, within the bounds of any type of structure, by such symbols as differences in qualifications, education and Party membership.

Moreover, youth structure as a whole and in each separate group is distinguished by its own internal demographic symbols (sex, age, family status, etc.) which also express certain features of its vital activity and social portrait.

The methodological principles of defining and analysing youth structure fully apply to rural youth. In its social class make-up, rural youth may be divided into collective-farm youth, worker (state-farm) youth and youth belonging to the stratum of the Soviet intelligentsia. It is not yet possible to give precise quantitative data for each of the groups by educational structure. But, the existing statistics on class structure in our society, on the rural population and farm personnel enable us to make an approximate evaluation of rural youth by social class characteristics. We know that some 10 million young men and women are presently engaged in collective or state farming[11]. That comprises about one third of the total number of people employed in agriculture. In 1970, of the 29 million farm workers, 17 million people worked on collective farms and 9.8 million on state farms[12]. Of the aggregate number of collective and state farm workers, about one million were members of the intelligentsia. Further, 60 per cent of that intelligentsia takes part in state farm production, and 40 per cent in collective farm work. If we assume that every third agricultural worker is a young person, then collective farm youth makes up approximately six million people, and state farm youth over three million, not including those who work at other state enterprises and establishments. In our surveys, the sample total corresponds to these objective indicators. The collective farm youth comprises 49 per cent, state farm youth 32 per cent, and young employees 15 per cent. Four per cent of our sample did not indicate their social affiliation.

In regard to labour activity and occupation, we divided rural youth into the following groups: 53.3 per cent in farm production; 6.3 per cent in local industrial work; 2.4 per cent in transport and building; 3.5 per cent in services; and 2.7 per cent in state and scientific establishments. A large percentage of the youngest members were schoolchildren in the senior forms -- 29 per cent.

Since our work was concerned mainly with young people engaged in collective or state farm production, we needed to obtain a more complete picture by more accurately differentiating young people by such socially significant features as production functions and the content and character of their work. We took as a basic element of structure the various occupationsl groups which contained the major social features alongside a similarity in labour content: trade, wages, education, level of social and political activity, and so on. We defined a total of nine occupational groups on the basis of classification according to degree of mental and manual labour, skilled and unskilled work. They included:

1. administrative and managerial personnel at top and medium levels -- 2 per cent;
2. specialists -- 3 per cent;
3. employees (without special education) -- 5 per cent

4. machine-operators -- 21 per cent;

5. people servicing farm machinery -- 3 per cent;

6. stockmen -- 15 per cent;

7. people doing non-mechanised work but possessing a trade (field-workers, gardeners, bee-keepers, etc.) -- 4 per cent;

8. builders -- 3 per cent;

9. people doing non-mechanised physical labour, not possessing a trade -- 34 per cent.

For comparative purposes, we added a group of industrial workers from among rural youth -- 5 per cent of the sample total.

The statistics on occupational groups of employed youth testify to the fact that it is engaged in socially useful work in all major sectors of production. At the same time, the statistics show the overall changes in the structure of Soviet society caused by social and scientific and technical progress. The changes in youth structure are well marked in all occupational groups.

Administrative and managerial personnel. This occupational group includes farm managers and all sub-divisions within the farm.

Our research results indicate that 51 per cent of young managers at all levels of production possess a higher or complete secondary education, of whom 31 per cent have a special secondary, incomplete higher or higher education. All the same, a substantial number of young people in leading positions still do not have a high enough level of education. This is particularly apparent at the junior and intermediate levels of managerial personnel (brigadiers, section, farm and sub-section managers). A further improvement in the education of young managerial personnel on collective and state farms is a very urgent problem; it can have a considerable effect on the social development of this group and the maturity of its structure.

Our results show that young people performing managerial duties work more intensively than any other occupational group to raise their educational level. Thirteen per cent of managers study in agricultural colleges and *tekhnikums*. A substantial group (37 per cent) is studying the humanities, largely economics;

eight per cent of managers are completing their education at school. Thus, virtually 60 per cent of managers among the youth are studying in various educational institutions.

The work service of managerial and administrative personnel also varies. The bulk of managers have been engaged in farming for over five years (55 per cent); 13 per cent have been working for less than a year, while 15 per cent -- from one to three years. We should point out that young managers are mainly people in the 24-30 age range (79 per cent) -- i.e., persons possessing considerable experience.

Party membership further testifies to the experience and maturity of young managerial personnel: 39 per cent are either candidate-members or full members of the Communist Party, and 34 per cent are Komsomol members.

Specialist group. This group contains representatives both of the rural production intelligentsia (agronomists, livestock experts, veterinary surgeons and engineers) and the non-production intelligentsia (teachers, doctors, etc.). Science and improved farm techniques exert a constant influence on the development and formation of this group. The rapid increase in the number of highly-skilled personnel in the village is a typical feature of mature socialism and the ongoing structural changes in society overall. In the last decade alone, the number of experts has doubled in collective, state and subsidiary farming. In December, 1960, the specialist group numbered 406,000, while by 1971 it had risen to 821,000.

The proportion of young people among specialists is impressive. Over 40 per cent of the collective and state farm experts are young people under 30; they generally have high educational standards, as the following table shows (in percentages):

Table 1: Education Levels of Young Collective and State Farmers (%)

Primary	5-6 Classes	7-8 Classes	Incomplete Secondary	Secondary	Secondary Special	Incomp. Higher	Higher
-	-	6	4	15	45	11	19

As Table 1 shows, 90 per cent of young specialists have secondary, secondary special or higher education.

Furthermore, 75 per cent of young specialists have been working for up to five years; 47 per cent of them are under 24 years of age. In other words, the overwhelming number of young specialists do not have a very long work record. This fact naturally demands particular attention from rural Komsomol organisations and more concern for higher qualifications and proficiency among young experts.

Machine-operators. Rural machine-operators are one of the largest occupational groups of skilled physical workers; they are changing both quantitatively and qualitatively in pace with the industrialisation of farming and the socialisation of labour.

The proportion of such personnel engaged in agriculture was 4.8 per cent in 1950, 9.8 per cent in 1960 and 13.9 by 1970. On April 1, 1971, the number of machine operators (tractor and lorry drivers, combine harvester drivers, chauffeurs) amounted to 3,503,000, that is, it had increased by 2.1 times since 1950[13]. The annual increase amounted on average to 5.1 per cent during this period. This shows the overall trend towards the technical re-equipment of farming and its impact on the changing occupational structure in agriculture as a whole and the youth structure in particular.

The main growth in machine-operators is now taking place through an influx of young people; this has been particularly great in recent years due to the mass campaign by the Leninist Komsomol to persuade rural youth to learn a machinist trade. During the first year of the Ninth Five-Year Plan, more than a million young men and women studied at trade schools, by correspondence courses or in universal training machinist groups.

At the present time, the share of young people among machine-operators is considerably greater than it is of older people. Thus, the number of tractor drivers, combine-harvester drivers and chauffeurs over 30, according to our research and that of Novosibirsk sociologists, is approximately 35 per cent, while it is 45.3 per cent for the 16-30 age group[14]. Young people make up an absolute majority of machine-operators in some farm sectors. All the same, we must remember that this young group is fairly diverse both in educational level and in work experience (See Table 2).

Table 2: Distribution of Young Machine-Operators by Education and Work Record, with Account for Age (%)

AGE GROUPS	EDUCATION								WORK RECORD				
	Primary	5-6 Classes	7-8 Classes	Incomplete Secondary	Secondary General	Secondary Special	Incomplete Higher	Higher	Up to 1 year	1-3 years	Up to 5 years	Up to 10 years	Over 10 years
Machine-Operators (all)...........	4	13	50	16	12	3.5	0.5	-	17	27	19	21	13
17-19...........	-	5	58	21	13	3	---	-	48	42	6	--	--
20-23...........	3	15	40	17	18	6	2	-	11	37	33	12	2
24-26...........	3	16	56	13	9	2	---	-	4	18	23	33	13
27 and over......	9	22	46	5	8	4	---	-	--	10	16	37	37

The Table shows that the level of skill of machine-operators greatly depends on their age-group. While the educational level is higher in the first two age groups, the next two (24-26 and 27 plus) are conspicuous for the great work experience and lower educational level. It is apparent that there is a general tendency for education to rise from the oldest group in relation to all the others. This gives us grounds to assume that in the near future there will be a levelling up and improvement in the education of machine operators in all age groups, which is an important condition for a successful mastery of trade experience in tune with the requirements of current scientific and technical progress.

Stockmen. We include in this group herdsmen, milkmaids, shepherds and other persons engaged in livestock breeding. Most of them are engaged in manual physical labour which presupposes a large group of people. Until recently, this work accounted for almost a fifth of all rural workers. Today, 15 per cent of rural youth are engaged in livestock handling. The persistent low level of technical equipment in livestock handling is reflected in the structure of young people working here (see Table 3).

Table 3: Distribution of Young Stockmen by Education and Work Record, Depending on Age and Sex (%)

	EDUCATION								WORK RECORD				
AGE GROUPS	Primary	5-6 Classes	7-8 Classes	Incomplete Secondary	Secondary General	Secondary Special	Incomplete Higher	Higher	Up to 1 year	1-3 years	Up to 5 years	Up to 10 years	Over 10 years
All stockmen...	8	19	53	10	9	0.5	--	--	16	21	16	27	18
Women under 19.	-	11	62	7	22	---	--	--	54	33	10	--	--
Women 20-23....	5	9	60	17	10	2	--	--	6	38	35	19	--
Women 24-26....	11	20	55	10	4	1	--	--	2	4	32	51	8
Women 27 plus..	14	18	52	8	3	-	--	--	3	11	10	36	34
Men under 26...	7	20	51	10	12	1	--	--	23	23	7	30	10
Men 27 plus....	25	26	41	2	2	--	--	--	2	8	5	26	55

Here, too, is an evident tendency for educational levels to rise in the direction of younger age groups, in so far as the influx of rural youth is now becoming quite normal. This is being encouraged both by the appearance of new technical operations, particularly at livestock complexes, and by the mechanisation of individual operations -- milking, water supply, fodder provision and clearning of buildings at existing and new farms. The changing structure of the livestock-handling group and their rising educational standards will increasingly depend on the mechanisation and automation of their work, because a young person now starting work in livestock handling is quite ready to handle such techniques, judging by his present educational level.

Non-mechanised manual group (without a speciality). Young people in this group make up a third of all young people employed in agriculture. But, within the group as a whole, they make up only half those over 30 years of age. For the moment, however, they remain the most numerous (34 per cent). This fact, as well as characterising the status of rural youth, also defines the attitude of young people to farming as a whole. Table 4 shows how the group is divided by age.

Table 4: Age Distribution of the Non-Mechanised Manual Group (%)

MEN				WOMEN			
Up to 19	20-23	24-26	27 and over	Up to 19	20-23	24-26	27 and over
42	13	17	28	30	18	21	31

Boys and girls under 19 comprise the greatest proportion; then the share sharply diminishes. This is particularly marked with men. In the next two age groups (24-26 and 27 and over), there is a stable trend for a growing proportion of young people.

Now let us turn to the educational characteristics of this group (see Table 5).

Table 5: Educational Levels in the Non-Mechanised Manual Group

AGE GROUPS	EDUCATION					
	Primary	5-6 Classes	7-8 Classes	Incomplete Secondary	Secondary General	Incomplete Secondary Special
Men up to 19	-	3	57	12	21	-
Men 20-23	-	9	43	9	31	6
Men 24-26	20	35	31	2	8	2
Men 27 plus	31	25	33	4	4	-
Women up to 19	3	8	35	24	29	1
Women 20-23	5	7	56	9	22	3
Women 24-26	8	16	58	11	5	1
Women 27 plus	12	22	50	3	9	1

The first two age groups (up to 19 and 20-23) have a fairly high educational level, even higher than for machine-operators and livestock handlers. The following two groups show a sharp decline in educational level which may be explained by the exceptional mobility of people in this group.

The group overall has a rather unique transfer-point from which young people move after training to a new and higher level of work. It is also useful in that it supplements all other occupational groups; it also contains potential migrants out of farming.

Thus, when we put the question "Are you thinking of moving to the town?", almost half the group said that they would prefer to work and live in the town. Yet the same group could provide a regular pool of labour supplying the village with skilled personnel if care were taken over every young person. This care must primarily be for acquiring a trade and improving qualifications.

The work records of young people in this group present a motley picture (see Table 6).

Table 6: Work Record of Non-Specialist Rural Youth(%)

AGE GROUPS	WORK RECORD				
	Up to 1 year	From 1 to 3 years	Up to 5 years	Up to 10 years	Over 10 years
Men up to 19	45	45	3	-	-
Men 20-23	9	34	28	15	6
Men 24-26	-	22	15	40	22
Men 27 plus	-	4	5	23	63
Women up to 19	47	32	12	-	-
Women 20-23	7	41	26	18	-
Women 24-26	1	3	13	45	31
Women 27 plus	1	4	9	20	64

Comparatively small groups of young people with specialist qualifications include construction workers and those concerned with farm machinery. They may be described as being closest to machine-operators and possess roughly the same educational level and work record. These, undoubtedly, are the prospective professional groups.

Young people at school or college occupy an important place in the rural youth structure and deserve special mention.

We attempted to gather information on the value and trade orientations of these young people and their life-plans. To this end we studied mainly rural school-leavers. Of the 1,800 schoolchildren in the eighth or tenth class of school who made up our sample, 48 per cent were boys and 52 girls; 71 per cent were school-leavers in the eighth class, 29 per cent in the tenth class. Most (54 per cent) were members of the Komsomol.

A description of the present-day rural youth structure would be incomplete without attention to such demographic factors as sex, age and family status. Although men comprised 49.5 per cent and women 50.5 per cent, this discrepancy accords with the overall statistical distribution of the rural population by sex throughout the country within the 15-30 age bracket.

The different age groups among employed rural youth are represented in Table 7.

Table 7: Distribution of Age-Groups Among Rural Youth (%)

14-16	17-19	20-23	24-26	27-30
3	26	18	24	29

These figures show that young rural workers are distributed comparatively evenly emong all the given age groups (the first group is not important in that it represents schoolchildren).

Investigation of family status produced the following results (see Table 8).

Table 8: Family Status of Rural Youth (%)

Unmarried	Married	Divorced	Not Given
44	45	1	10

This distribution indicates that almost half the young people have independent families. Further, 49 per cent of the families have children: 25 per cent have one child, 18 per cent - two, 6 per cent - three or more. These figures show a stable trend towards the strengthening of young families in the countryside.

An analysis of the rural youth structure is important both for economic activity and for the communist socialisation of young people. Scientific information about each separate youth group helps us take more purposeful action in work with young people, gain a more concrete understanding of youth problems and guarantees a comparability of scientific and practical results. Specific information obtained from social and occupational groupings, education and age necessitates different approaches to tackling overall issues associated with communist education.

Further changes in youth structure and its social position depend on the general economic and cultural situation in the Soviet village. It is therefore vital to elucidate the specific features of the development that is creating new working and living conditions for rural youth.

CHAPTER TWO

WORKING AND LIVING CONDITIONS OF SOVIET RURAL YOUTH

1. Material and technological basis of farming

Far reaching social, economic, political and cultural changes have taken place in the Soviet village during the years of socialist construction; they have radically altered the destinies of rural youth and transformed the very basis of its formation -- peasant labour.

As a result of the implementation of Lenin's co-operative plan, hitherto-backward agriculture became a large-scale mechanised and advanced socialist system of farming. Lenin's dream became reality: "to transform agriculture from an unconciously-conducted, old-fashioned affair into an enterprise founded on science and technical achievements"[1]. The time is gone forever when a peasant had to work his tiny homestead in blindness and ignorance, stultified by every condition of life, when his labour was wholly linked to the use of primitive implements on a small patch of land.

The Soviet peasant has the benefit of team work organised along socialist lines in new social circumstances; he has overcome the age-old force of habit of the petty proprietor, he has developed commonsense virtues and changed his psychology. "Work in a collective farm based on scientific and technological achievements has altered the spiritual outlook of the peasant. He now exhibits team-work, a keen sense of social duty, loyalty to the great Leninist ideals and a high degree of labour and political activity."[2] Nowadays the Soviet village operates under mature socialism; this historical situation reflects both the major attainments of the past and the new opportunities, the future prospects for transforming rural life and peasant labour. Mature socialism, as noted at the 24th Party Congress, is characterised by the all-round and harmonious development of economic, social, political and cultural conditions. At this stage, L.I. Brezhnev has said, we can and must resolve simultaneously a wider range of economic, social and political tasks[3].

In recent years, the Communist Party has elaborated an extensive, long-term and realistic programme of agricultural development. It embraces a whole range of factors designed to stimulate farm production; they include supplying the countryside with necessary technology and fertilisers, expanding capital construction, ameliorating the soil, training manpower and improving the organisation of production.

To be successful, the programme envisages above all a substantial improvement in the material and technological base, so that all branches of farming are supplied with modern scientific and technological equipment. Brezhnev again: "In tackling the current tasks that face us, we must simultaneously during the Five-Year Plan period take a big step forward in creating a material and technological base in agriculture which will help us to resolve completely the problems of farm production and to transform the village, to reduce dependence on the elements."[4] For these purposes, special capital investment has been earmarked for agriculture. During the current Five-Year Plan, the sum of 129,000 million roubles has been invested in farming -- i.e., an amount equivalent to that invested in agriculture in the previous two five-year periods together. New capital investment is primarily being directed into industrialising farm production -- into full-scale mechanisation, automation and electrification, construction of repair bases and land-amelioration schemes.

The rate of the technical equipment of agriculture has been constantly rising. By early 1971, the total number of tractors was 4,343,000 (estimated on 15 power), trucks and lorries - 1,206,000 and combine harvesters - 623,000[5]. Over the 1971-1975 span, collective and state farms were to receive another 1,700,000 tractors, 1,100,000 trucks and lorries, 831,000 combine harvesters, 6,000 million roubles worth or machinery for mechanised work in livestock breeding and much other machinery.

A typical feature of farm improvement today is not simply the wholesale use of technical equipment, but the considerable range of machinery being employed. We shall soon be manufacturing some 1,400 different types of plant machinery. Over half is already in commission. Back in 1928, Soviet industry produced only 67 types of simple farm machinery, in 1940 -- 112 types, and in 1970 -- nearly 800 types. While our first tractors on steel wheels had a field-speed of 3-4 km. p.h., and were only slightly faster on transport work, today's tractors with pneumatic tyres do field-work at a speed of 5-9 km. p.h., and travel almost as fast as motor cars in transporting loads. More and more farms are being supplied with K-700 tractors with 220 h.p. engines. The operating speed of this tractor is up to 16 km.p.h. on field work and 31 km.p.h. on transport work. In power, reliability, handling and hardiness, modern tractors bear no comparison with those of the 1930's and 1940's. With the aid of today's machinery, it is possible to guarantee comprehensive mechanisation of the cultivation and harvesting of grain, maize, sugar-beet, potatoes, flax and fodder crops in the major arable zones of the country.

The Soviet countryside received over a million different items of electrically-driven farm machinery in the five years 1966-1970; the use of electricity and internal combustion engines is likely to increase in future. Table 9 testifies to the changes in power resources on collective and state farms over recent years.

Table 9: Power Capacity of Agriculture (end of year; mln.h.p.)[6]

Indicator	1916	1940	1950	1960	1965	1966	1967	1968	1969	1970
Total power capacity........	23.9	47.5	62.3	155.9	236.6	250.1	266.9	280.2	305.2	336.4
Mechanical engines.........	0.2	36.9	55.0	151.2	232.9	246.5	263.4	276.3	302.0	333.3
Draught animals (estimated as mechanical power).........	23.7	10.6	7.3	4.7	3.7	3.6	3.5	3.9	3.2	3.1

Between 1940 and 1970, the power capacity of collective and state farms thus increased more than seven-fold. From 1940 to 1950, it grew on average by 1,500,000 h.p. annually, between 1950 and 1960, it was 9,300,000 h.p. annually;

during the 1960's, the average annual increment was approximately 16,000,000 h.p.[7].

Between 1971 and 1975, it is intended to increase this to 161,000,000 h.p., or by one and a half times -- i.e., it will amount to some 500,000,000 h.p. This will change fundamentally the position of the rural worker. Before the Revolution, in the period 1913-1917, each peasant had about 0.5 h.p. of electric energy; in 1960, he had 5.4 h.p. and, in 1971, as much as 11.2 h.p. During the Soviet years, therefore, electric energy per agricultural worker has increased more than 22 times. It was not so long ago that the peasant considered himself the basic elemental force in the labour process, inasmuch as he was the source of energy and performed all the labour operations, using only primitive implements. Now, these functions are increasingly being transferred to machines. This is strikingly apparent in figures showing the correlation of men to machines over the last hundred years[8].

Table 10: Correlation of Men to Machines in Agriculture, Selected Years, 1850-1960

Share in the labour process	SELECTED YEARS			
	1850	1900	1930	1960
Man...........	15	10	4	4
Animal........	79	52	12	1
Machine.......	6	38	84	96

Electrification of all branches of agriculture has brought far-reaching changes in farm working conditions. At the turn of the century, Lenin had foreseen the gigantic victory of large-scale production, gained from the introduction of power technology into farming; he underlined its advantages in all manner of farming operations[9]. In the latter years of his life, he frequently returned to this issue; thus, he wrote in 1920: 'We know how to ensure the basis of communism in agriculture -- it can be done by an enormous technological evolution. We clearly envisage this plan with local power stations; we have mapped out the minimum programme."[10]

Experts tell us that we can use electricity in as many as 700 farming processes. At present, it is employed only in 70 -- i.e., 10 per cent of total capacity. It is not difficult to appreciate how greatly the whole nature and conditions of work will change in the near future.

Use of electricity in the countryside is constantly on the increase (see Table 11).

Table 11: Power Consumption in Agriculture, Selected Years, 1928-1970[11]

INDICATOR	1928	1940	1950	1960	1965	1966	1967	1968	1969	1970
Total electric-power consumption in agriculture (mln. kwt.)........	35	538	1538	9970	21099	23209	25754	29248	33256	38552
Number of collective farms using electric power (as % of total no. of coll. farms)	--	-	15	71	95	97	99	99.4	99.7	99.8
Number of state farms using electric power (as % of total no. of state farms)	--	-	76	98	99	99	99.5	99.7	99.7	99.8

Table 11 shows how rapidly the rate of rural power consumption has been rising. The farms had some two million electric motors in 1966 and almost five million by the end of 1970. Over half the farms now have 100 or more electric motors, and some have between 500 and 800 each. In 1970, Soviet agriculture received 38,000 million kilowatt hours of electricity, which was to double, to 75,000 million kwh by 1975[12]. That would make it possible to increase the use of electricity in all areas of farm work and to improve living conditions in the Soviet village.

Amelioration of the soil and the application of chemicals are also increasingly important. Chemicalisation of farming is just one aspect of the scientific and technological revolution, ensuring a rapid growth in farm output. It is a major means of improving soil fertility and crop yield. We used 27 million tonnes of mineral fertiliser in farming in 1965 and 46 million in 1970; this was to rise to 75 million by 1975. We now have an elaborate programme of farming chemicalisation on the basis of data from agro-chemical science which defines the country's requirements for mineral fertilisers, their distribution among crop groups and natural economic regions; it gives a detailed description of the application of mineral and organic fertiliser in various zones of the country.

Academician V. Pannikov estimates from several experimental investigations that the effectiveness of mineral fertiliser, expressed in farm output increases per centner of standard fertiliser, is as follows: from 1.1 to 1.4 centners for grain, from 0.2 to 0.3 for flax, from 0.6 to 1.0 for cotton, from 4.4 to 7.8 for sugar beet, from 9 to 11 for silo maize, and up to 5 centners for clover (for hay)[13]. Thus, an extra four centners of grain should be obtained from every hectare by 1975 -- mainly through transforming farming technology and applying chemicals.

Amelioration projects today embrace all zones and are an effective means of conserving and augmenting soil fertility. This conforms with Lenin's plea, in November 1917, "to care for the land like the apple of your eye -- it is the people's wealth"[14].

Areas requiring irrigation made a consequent gain of almost a twenty per cent in field area during the five-year period up to 1970; collective and state farms received an extra 1,500,000 hectares of irrigated land. Moreover, the farms themselves brought into use another 300,000 hectares. An even more ambitious project is being implemented during the 1971-75 plan period. State investment is to bring three million hectares of irrigated land into use by 1975 and to dry out five million hectares in over-humid areas. It is also envisaged watering some 41,200,000 hectares of pasture land and increasing the existing irrigated lands. The state has earmarked over 26,000 million roubles for amelioration work during the current five-year period[15]. For the first time in the history of our country, we shall create large areas for cultivating grain on irrigated fields. Thus, some 10-12 million tonnes of grain are to be obtained from irrigated lands in 1975.

Reclaimed land constitutes an immense wealth. While occupying only five per cent of the land under plough -- some seventeen million hectares -- it accounts for almost one fifth of gross farm production, including almost all the cotton, 97 per cent of the rice, three-fifths of the vegetables and a considerable proportion of the fruit, grapes, melon and other crops[16]. Every hectare of irrigated land is a truly golden hectare which, given proper technical standards, can yield 40-50 centners of wheat, 50-60 centners of rice and 35-40 centners of cotton.

The development of comprehensive mechanisation, electrification and chemicalisation of farm production is radically altering the character of peasant labour, making new demands on professional and general training. As L.I. Brezhnev put it in his speech at the 16th Komsomol Congress, successful agricultural intensification is "only possible with people who are technically literate, skilled, who love and cherish the land"[17].

Traditional jobs are changing and being carried out on a higher specialist level. In livestock handling, for example, new specialist jobs are appearing -- shepherd-mechanic, automatic milking specialist, sheep-shearing specialist, fodder work-shop operator, servicer of automatic drinking equipment and of inter-farm transport, etc. Such low-grade jobs as ploughmen and seeders are gradually dying out.

Not only are old jobs fading away; the range of agricultural trades is greatly being extended. One of the largest groups in farming today is that concerned with servicing machinery: fitters, turners, vulcanisers, etc. With the increased use of electric power, the number of electricians, radio technicians and electric welders is rising fast; chemicalisation is giving a boost to agricultural chemists. Farming currently employs over one hundred trades, most of which are mechanised.

The differentiation of jobs caused by the increasing division of labour is linked up with the integration of work, the combination of different jobs and trades which are more or less similar in their labour functions. In several mechanised trades, there is an evident trend towards a single person combining several specialisms in a single technological cycle. Our survey of mechanised work reveals that every other worker possesses two or more trades. For example, the tractor-mechanic effectively combines several trades.

These processes are bound to attract youth. Furthermore, improved and modernised farming considerably depends on the more creative participation of young people, on their energy and enthusiasm, their all-round creative endeavour stimulated by socialist conditions. The selfless work of rural youth and the mass movement to master a technical trade are a vivid example of its involvement in these processes, in scientific and technological progress and the further expansion of agriculture.

2. Importance of improved rural living and cultural conditions

The village today is characterised by mounting material and cultural well-being, providing every opportunity for people to manifest labour and social initiative.

Clear evidence of this process is the growth in the real incomes of farm workers, distributed on the socialist principle of material rewards for the quantity and quality of labour expended and by means of a substantial increase in the public consumption funds.

Between 1917 and 1967, the cash and income in kind of peasants from farming (with account for free education and health treatment, pensions, allowances and other payments and state emoluments) rose 8.5 times[18]. In 1970, an average of 3 roubles 90 kopecks was paid per man-day on collective farms -- which is more than double the labour-day payments of 1960.

If we turn to another group of farm workers -- those on state farms -- we gain some idea of the increase in their real earnings from wage increases over the last thirty years (see Table 12).

Table 12: Average Monthly Earnings in the USSR, Selected Years, 1940 - 1970 (rbls.)[19]

Indicator	1940	1960	1965	1966	1967	1968	1969	1970
Entire economy	33.1	80.6	96.5	100.2	104.7	112.7	116.9	122.0
State farms	22.0	53.8	74.6	80.0	84.4	92.1	93.2	100.9

Not only is there a constant rise in state farmers' incomes, there is also a trend towards a levelling out of their incomes and average wages for the economy as a whole. In the last decade alone, these income differentials have been halved: from 33 per cent in 1960 to 17 per cent in 1970. As much as 4 roubles 43 kopecks was paid on average to state farm employees in 1970 per man-day.

The public consumption funds are of increasing significance in the rising rural living standards. Farmers now receive free medical treatment, free education and trade training, student grants, various state allowances, pensions, holidays with pay and several other state emoluments. These have increased more than 50-fold per collective farmer during Soviet times (see Table 13).

Table 13: State Payments to the Population from Public Consumption Funds (rbls.)[20]

State Payments	1940	1960	1965	1966	1967	1968	1969	1970
Total (thous. mln.)...........	4.6	27.3	41.9	45.5	49.4	55.3	59.7	63.9
Per capita......	24	127	182	195	209	232	248	263

The importance of public consumption funds to young people is very great. They ensure free schooling, paid holidays and allowances, child maintenance in nursery schools, favourable holiday facilities, etc. Thus, almost half the vouchers to rest homes and santoria in the farms we surveyed go to persons under 30. Young parents now have excellent opportunities for leaving children in nurseries.

According to our research, in which all age groups of farm workers are represented, the average monthly earnings of young people (excluding the first age group) are somewhat higher than both the average and that of older age groups (see Table 14).

Table 14: Average Monthly Earnings of Farm Workers, by Age Group(rbls.)

N.B. The table contains data of research carried out by the laboratory in 1969. Indices are given in percentages.

Age	Up to 60	61-80	81-100	101-120	121-150	Over 150
Total....	19	29	25	15	7	3
18-19....	11	35	41	8	5	-
20-23....	10	32	29	18	10	1
24-26....	10	31	23	15	12	4
27-30....	14	32	25	14	9	6
31-35....	11	30	27	19	8	3
36-40....	16	24	30	20	7	3
41-45....	15	33	27	13	7	3
46-50....	16	38	21	14	6	4
51-55....	20	36	22	14	4	4
56-60....	33	27	21	11	4	2

The higher monthly average earnings for young people in the 20-30 age group is largely due, in our view, to their employment in more skilled trades than other farm workers. Young people have ample opportunities to acquire a skilled trade. Thus, as many as 794,000 persons were trained in mechanised trades in 1970 out of all rural youth[21]. These circumstances naturally have a favourable effect both on professional advancement and on material well-being. The new and progressive forms of labour payment are also having a positive effect on the material position of young people. The introduction, for example, of the piece-rate bonus payment system, as farmers themselves testify, reinforces the material situation not only through providing an opportunity of getting higher pay, but also through receiving a lump sum at the end of the farming year on the basis of the harvest. Over 70 per cent of the machine-operators in the survey drew attention to this fact. Of the 426 replies received during the survey, we reproduce just a few below, giving a fuller picture of this aspect of payment for the final product of collective labour.

"The piece-work payment is very valuable to us and the farm. A good harvest gained through working together is of benefit to me, to my family and to the farm. At the end of the year we get a lump sum as out of a money-box. My wife and I plan to use it to buy something expensive, go on holiday and have a good rest" (team-member K. Korablex, Novokubansky raion, Krasnodarsky krai).

"I am a young machine-operator. This is my third year in the team. In this time I have bought a motorbike, I dress well, and I am helped a great deal by the large pay-out at the end of the year" (team mechaniser N. Mochalov, Alexandrovsky raion, Stavropolsky krai).

"A big sum at the end of the year is a very good thing. All the members of our team now have TV sets, washing machines, radios, motorbikes or mopeds. The monthly advance is quite sufficient to cover food and clothes. And at the end of the year, when we get the money for the harvest, everyone thinks of buying something expensive" (team-member I. Khmelovsky, Millerovsky raion, Rostovskaya oblast).

The increasing remuneration and material welfare of Soviet villagers are today an irrefutable fact and provide good grounds for further growth. The 24th Congress Directives encompass a pay increase for collective farmers in the public sector of farming of 30-35 per cent in the 1971-75 period, and for state farmers of 20-22 per cent. All these measures will undoubtedly have a favourable effect on the material welfare of rural youth.

We should not conclude, however, that there are no problems in creating the necessary material conditions for involving young girls and boys in farming. We cannot agree with those sociologists who maintain that young people take a passive attitude to earnings as if they were of secondary importance. Such opinions often rely on the responses of schoolchildren or young people living with their parents, for whom earnings do not yet play such an important role. In actual fact, such factors as big fluctuations in seasonal earnings and a substantial number of low-paid jobs still remain important reasons for the exodus of young people from the villages.

Let us return to the figures in Table 14. They show that young people between 18 and 20 have average monthly earnings somewhat lower than the overall average indices. This is, of course, because they lack experience, knowledge and training. Many commence their work as low-skilled, low-paid manual workers. Yet it is precisely in these years that young people study most intensively, acquire knowledge and professional experience. Taking these factors into account, many farms have taken additional measures to help young people find their feet at the very outset to their careers. For example, at the Kirov Collective Farm in Orenburg oblast, secondary school-leavers and ex-National Servicemen receive a rate of pay ten per cent higher than the current payment rates for the first three years' work on the farm. Those who start work on the farm are given, gratis, a large sum of money; young married couples receive loans from the farm to build a house or a flat. Similar systems exist in the Altai krai and other areas of the country, helping young people to make a successful start in life.

The immense social and economic changes which have taken place have made far-reaching effects on the everyday life and culture of the village. Above all, they have altered the external appearance of the village. Virtually all tumbledown shacks and thatched dwellings, which were a common sight in villages since time immemorial, have disappeared.* The extensive building programme has changed the face of the village, particularly since the late 1950's. New schools and hospitals, trading centres and sports grounds have appeared amid well-appointed houses with iron and slate roofs. In the ten-year period (1960-70) alone, rural areas received an extra 402.6 million square metres of housing space[22]. The bulk of rural youth (79 per cent) live in their parents' houses or have their own homes. A further fifteen per cent reside in apartments belonging to farms, establishments or other organisations. And only six per cent, mostly specialists and employees, rent rooms.

The interior of a farmer's home has also greatly changed. The penetration of 'urban' features is marked in the character of the whole domestic situation: modern furniture, personal libraries, cultural and household equipment, and so on.

* This is not quite the case. (translator)

Table 15: Cultural and Household Equipment in Rural Homes
(% of People in Survey)

Radio	77	Wardrobe	66
Radio-and-recorder player	65	Bicycle	55
Television set	32	Motorcycle, moped	18
Camera	16	Motor car	2
Musical instrument	18	Vacuum cleaner	4
Sewing machine	62	Piano	3
Refrigerator	15	Sideboard	51

An exceptional trend is observable in these figures: changes are occurring not merely in the material equipment of the rural resident, they are affecting the whole tenor of rural life. The wide dissemination of the mass media is eroding the last outposts of the patriarchal system, is firmly binding every resident of even the most far-flung village to the life of our entire society. Cultural values are becoming accessible to all. In this way, we can clearly see life in the village coming closer to that in the town.

The 24th Congress Directives envisage a big increase in the supply of consumer goods to the village. Sales to the population are to increase by 80 per cent: "The supply of refrigerators per 100 families will rise from 32 in 1970 to 64 in 1975, TV sets from 51 to 72, washing machines from 52 to 72."[23] As shown by the results of our survey, carried out in the Kaluga region in 1972, the Directive target figures for 1975 for washing machines and TV sets are already being surpassed. As many as 73 per cent of all families have washing machines and 83 per cent have TV sets. Several areas of the country have, in fact, reached this target.

On the day that the Third All-Union Collective Farm Congress opened, Pravda wrote that "in four years (1965-68), the state has sold to rural localities 32,800,000 watches and clocks, 1,500,000 refrigerators, 1,400,000 motorcycles, 6,800,000 radios and 4,600,000 televisions. The annual trade turnover in the village is now reckoned to run into many millions of roubles"[24]. The rural inhabitant, particularly the young farmer, is now interested in seeing that the village stores are as good as any shop town, both in assortment of goods and in quality. Motorcycles, motor cars, gas-cylinder points, television, radios, refrigerators, vacuum cleaners, washing machines are all in heavy demand in the village.

Culture in the village has also changed out of all recognition. In tsarist Russia, more than three-quarters of the rural population was illiterate (the rural population accounted for in excess of 80 per cent of the people in the Russian Empire); rural illiteracy was far greater than in the towns -- the level of literacy among men was almost half, and among women 3.7 times less than what it was in the town[25].

As a consequence of fundamental social and economic change and the literacy-campaigns soon after the revolution, the percentage of literacy had more than doubled by the end of 1926. In 1939, a majority (87 per cent) was already literate. And by 1959, practically the entire population, 9-49, was literate (98.5 per cent). It is one of the greatest achievements of Soviet power that today more than half the rural population has completed secondary or higher education. In the last 30 years alone, the number of people with higher and secondary education (per thousand rural inhabitants) has increased more than 20 times. The social significance of these cultural indices is especially marked if we consider that in 1940 the number of people with secondary or higher education amounted to only six per cent of rural dwellers.

It is impossible to find anywhere in our country today any more or less sizeable settlement without its secondary school. The extensive network of schools and other educational establishments ensures favourable conditions for constant improvement in educational standards among rural youth.

Our research enables us to compare the educational levels of two generations: the young people who began their studies in the 1930's and 1940's, and contemporary young people. For a clearer picture of cultural change in the Soviet village, let us examine the educational standards for each professional group of young people separately (see Tables 16, 17 and 18).

Table 16: Educational Standards of Young Rural Specialists and of their Parents (%)

Indicator	Primary	5-6 Classes	7-8 Classes	Secondary General	Secondary Special	Incompl. Higher	Higher
Young rural specialists	-	-	6	19	45	11	19
Father	36	11	18	7	7	1	3.5
Mother	49	9	17	5	7	1	2

The educational differences, as apparent in the table, between young rural specialists and their parents are enormous. While only some sixteen per cent of parents have had an education as high as incomplete or complete secondary, the overwhelming majority of their children have completed secondary education.

No less divergent are the educational indicators among parents and children in other occupational groups.

Table 17: Educational Standards of Young Machine-Operators and of their Parents (%)

Indicator	Primary	5-6 Classes	7-8 Classes	Secondary General	Secondary Special	Incompl. Higher	Higher
Young machine-operator	4	13	50	13	4	1	-
Father	48	15	12	3	2	1	-
Mother	60	11	9	2	1	-	-

The figures in the previous table also reveal the essential differences between parents and children in regard to education. The educational standards of parents of young machine-operators are overwhelmingly lower than eight classes and are markedly lower than that of the parents of young specialists. Many of them possess only a primary education. Yet every sixth child in this group has secondary or special secondary education, and every other child has completed seven or eight classes.

Table 18: Educational Standards of Young Stockmen and of their Parents(%)

Indicator	Primary	5-6 Classes	7-8 Classes	Secondary General	Secondary Special	Incompl. Higher	Higher
Young stockmen	8	19	53	19	0.5	-	-
Father	56	9	6	1	1	-	-
Mother	71	6	4	0.5	-	-	-

In this group, the educational contrast between parents and children is even more striking. Approximately the same applies to the non-specialised and non-mechanised group.

A comparison of the educational standards of the two generations provides evident confirmation that enormous cultural changes have occurred in the countryside and that the educational training of the younger generation has improved considerably. Thanks to these changes, young people today enter upon their new life as more literate and better able to play a full part in tackling the complicated problems involved in bringing even greater transformations to farming and rural culture.

The extensive network of clubs, libraries and houses of culture is playing an important part in promoting culture in the countryside. Every year, more than nine million lectures are read to the rural population; this is largely to the credit of the rural cultural and enlightenment institutions. The clubs and houses of culture are the location of interesting meetings, a place to get together with one's friends and to pursue various artistic activities.

Unfortunately, judging by remarks on the work of clubs and houses of culture, many of them are not meeting the mounting requirements of young people. The Ninth Five-Yar Plan made plans for improving facilities in the various cultural establishments and to increase the number of clubs and libraries so as to create better conditions for rural culture.

Today, the factor of improving culture in the village is becoming a vital criterion of farm activity on a par with an evaluation of its economic achievements. For example, this approach is evident in the social programmes of many collective and state farms up and down the country. The social plans being put into effect by farms in the Tambov region contain ambitious cultural projects that occupy as prominent a place as issues concerning production. Moreover, their successful implementation is being associated with the participation of young people. Involvement of youth is regarded as a necessary condition for realising the plans. Such measures rely on the interest of young people and their experience in founding modern cultural places in the countryside. During the Eighth Five-Year Plan alone, young people had a direct hand in building some 12,000 clubs, 16,000 mobile film units, 350 cinemas and over 2,000 libraries. In this way a firm and wide basis is being created in the village for young people to demonstrate their abilities both in production and in other forms of socially-useful activity.

CHAPTER THREE

SOCIALLY-USEFUL WORK AS A SOCIAL ORIENTATION

1. Productive labour as the foundation of the lives of rural youth

Socialist labour is the basis of the formation of a new man and therefore plays an exceptionally important role in the lives of young people. For each successive generation of Soviet youth it acts as a mighty means of enrolling it in the great army of working people, of inculcating valuable personality attributes; it is a sphere of supplementing and developing abilities. Young people embody in their work Lenin's behest to forge from themselves real communists in selfless labour, togehter with workers and peasants, in common struggle for a new life.

The contribution of all generations of rural youth is important to the cause of the socialist transformation of the Soviet countryside. Their labour path has been hard but glorious.

Alongwith the rest of the population, rural youth brought about a revolution in the village in creating collective farming, mastering new techniques and bringing the first tractors into the fields. The 1930's marked the first mass campaign by young people of the village to acquire a technical trade. Of the 2,500,000 machine-operators trained between 1931 and 1934, 80 per cent were young people. The campaign to master a trade in those years was associated with the mass campaign for shock work, for the acquiring of technical knowledge by girls as well as boys, and it testifies to the massive changes in farm labour.

The whole country knows the labour exploits of the young initiators of the innovation movement in the countryside -- team-members Maria Demchenko and Maria Gnatchenko, the combine-harvester driver Konstantin Borin, the milk-maid Taisia Prokopieva, the tractor-driver Pasha Angelina who, in 1933, organised the first women's tractor brigade and inspired the setting up of similar brigades in other parts of the country. Thousands of girls responded to her patriotic call "A hundred thousand girl-friends -- to the tractors!" By the end of 1939, 200,000 women had acquired a trade as a machine-operator.

Young people have been to the fore in the campaigns of subsequent years, to increase productivity and to plough up the virgin lands; their efforts have been rewarded by the government, which has made thousands of young farmers Heroes of Socialist Labour.

All occupational groups of young people are currently helping to improve the efficiency of farming. But people who have already learned a trade -- machine-operators -- are today the central figures in putting farming onto a modern industrial foundation. As L.I. Brezhnev said at the Central Committee plenary meeting in July 1970, "the machine-operator is the central figure in the countryside. And we should surround him with attention, not begrudging efforts to reinforce such people in state and collective farms. Otherwise it will be difficult for us to resolve the tasks of improving farm production"[1].

A new social type of worker in the modern Soviet village is clearly emerging in the form of the machine-operator. His work involves sophisticated technology and techniques, and he holds a leading place in production. Although machine-operators account for only one sixth of those engaged in farming, they perform the greater part of all agricultural work. The extent of rational and high-productive work performed by the machine-operator very much decides the success or failure of the harvest, and the overall results of production on all farms.

The army of rural machine-operators is constantly growing, as we can see from the figures for growth between 1928 and 1971[2] (see Table 19).

Approximately every eighth collective farmer and every fifth state farmer are now operating machines.

The distribution in the countryside of machine-operating and other technical trades is having a profound effect on the fate of rural youth, is answering their requirements for creative, highly-skilled work and is having a marked effect on their attitudes to farm work. The trade of machine-operating is enjoying particular popularity among young people and has been growing in attraction in recent years because of the measures undertaken by the

Party. That is the reason for the high evaluation given to this type of work and its social status by machine-operators during our investigations.

Table 19: Machine-Operators in Collective and State Farms (thous.)

Indicator	1928	1940	1950	1960	1965	1970	1971
Tractor and combine-harvester drivers and chauffeurs.......	18.2	1401	1356	2579	3094	3443	3503
Of whom:							
in coll. farms...	10.8	1298	1230	1767	1876	2042	2068
in state farms...	7.4	103	126	812	1218	1401	1435
Of total:							
tractor and harvester drivers	17.5	1237	1182	1818	2245	2420	2449
chauffeurs.......	0.7	164	174	761	849	1023	1054

Attitudes to and evaluation of one's own work primarily depend on the extent to which a person is satisfied with the nature and results of productive activity and his role in the group. Work satisfaction is, in our opinion, the best general index of socialist social relations. It combines the meaning and conditions of work, the way it is organised and remunerated both materially and morally, the so-called psychological atmosphere of the work team. With this high criterion we approached both the question of how satisfied machine-operators and other trades were with their work, and an explanation for motives and orientations for particular types of work.

In response to the question "Are you content with your work?" machine-operators in all the age groups we defined provided us with a fairly firm guide, as Table 20 indicates.

Table 20: "Are You Content with Your Work?" (%)

Indicator	Entire Sample	Machine-Operators (Age)			
		17-19	20-23	24-26	27-29
Very content	40	47	43	41	49
Satisfied	43	39	42	48	44
Indifferent	3	2	4	4	2
Dissatisfied	7	6	6	4	4
Dislike	2	2	3	1	-
No reply	5	4	2	2	1

Evidently, 83 per cent of machine-operators favourably evaluate their trade. Nonetheless, all these answers of a general nature. We therefore deemed it necessary to have a follow-up survey to examine in what ways respondents thought their work interesting (See Table 21).

In substantiating satisfaction with their work, machine-operators make special mention of the content of their trade, its creative potential, social significance, the role of the team and good relations with friends. Another feature is also noteworthy: while work-satisfaction by creative potential rises from the younger to the older group (13 and 25 per cent respectively), it reamins virtually the same, relatively high (18-19 per cent), for all age groups in regard to social significance. The latter bears witness, in our opinion, to the high degree of civic responsibility and political awareness of young rural machine-operators, therefore, that about half of the operators say that they chose their trade themselves and that it accords with their aspirations. When we asked why they chose their trade, only sixteen per cent of the machine-operators said they had no other choice and regarded it as temporary work. In all other cases (84 per cent), the choice was made on the basis of positive motivation.

Table 21: "What Attracts You in the Work You Do"? (%)

Indicator	AGE			
	17-19	20-23	24-26	27-30
Interesting trade, speciality....................	26	35	32	33
I like farm work and the chance to work in the open air........	29	26	28	15
The work requires sharpness and discipline.....................	13	18	21	25
I like the importance of farm work............................	18	18	18	18
I like the team in which I work	15	13	18	18
I like the pay.................	5	10	12	16
Good, friendly relations with companions...................	10	7	11	13
The work is not tiring.........	8	5	6	6

The machine-operators obviously value the strong influence of the team and good relations with work-mates as measures of work-satisfaction.

Particularly marked is the favourable effect of team-work on young people; this can be seen in the responses of members of such teams. Young machine-operators refer to the great importance of team-work to the lives of every team-member as well as to improving the organisation and efficiency of work. Some of the most frequently met replies were the following: "The team helped me get a trade", "I learned to work in the team", "The collective set me on my feet" and, even, "The team saved me". The teams certainly seem to have that 'psychological atmosphere', referred to earlier, when members work well together, breathe freely and live in harmony.

Good and friendly relations have taken shape in nearly all teams, according to machine-operators, and this helps them at work, rest, study and in the home. Virtually 90 per cent of the respondents evaluate mutual relationships in their teams as smooth, comradely and harmonious; nine per cent called them more or less as expected and only two per cent were dissatisfied.

The degree of work-satisfaction may also be measured when machine-operators rate their position in social production as a whole. Here we can judge the extent to which a person appreciates his duty and responsibility for the common cause, the extent to which he considers himself involved in resolving all the tasks of the collective or state farm. This valuable quality is expressed in the feeling among Soviet people of being masters of their own fate or, to be more precise, joint masters of socialist production.

The machine-operators acquire their responsibility in agricultural production. They invariably link work-satisfaction with an awareness that they really are genuine masters of the land, guardians of the collective and state farm fields. When we asked whether people felt themselves masters of their work, most young machine-operators answered in the affirmative (though we should point out that we had twenty per cent more affirmative replies among the self-accounting work teams).

All age groups among machine-operators gave a high rating to their position in the teams; but there is a general tendency for the older groups to rate their status in the collective higher. This is borne out by the rating given by the group directly.

When we asked how people rated their work, we took into consideration both personal judgements and objective characteristics such as participation in agricultural exhibitions and certain forms of moral rewards. Table 22 shows with greater clarity the work records of machine-operators and their level of skill.

Table 22: "How do you Rate Your Work?" (%) (By Age, Work Record and Grading of Machine-Operators)

INDICATOR	AGE					WORK RECORD			GRADING		
	18 - 20	21 - 23	24 - 26	27 - 30	31 - 35	Up to a Year	2 - 3 Years	4 Years or More	3rd	2nd	1st
I am a front-line worker................	22	30	36	39	46	26	44	58	35	49	57
I have diplomas, bonuses for my work...	30	31	37	37	47	25	45	57	37	51	53
I have government honours..............	2	3	5	6	15	4	11	25	6	18	27
I have taken part in agricultural exhibitions..........	4	4	6	9	11	5	6	17	4	7	22
I am not yet ranked among the best workers in my team....	18	15	12	9	9	15	6	9	12	11	8
I have had reprimands and punishments for slackness.............	3	3	6	4	2	3	2	1	3	3	1

N.B. The table includes data obtained from a survey among machine-operator teams

The Table reveals that the older the group the higher the level of public recognition. This fact is confirmed by work-rating indices depending on work record and grading in which, of course, the senior age groups possess higher skill and a longer work record.

The major index of wage-payments in work-satisfaction also bears out this conclusion. While we found that dissatisfaction with pay is still fairly high (eighteen per cent) among 17-20 year olds, it is considerably lower -- from eight to twelve per cent -- among the older groups.

All these facts, caused largely by lack of experience and knowledge among the youngest machine-operators, demand the most careful and constant consideration in training young personnel. This is all the more important because there are many other factors which have an adverse effect on work-satisfaction and hamper the improvement of conditions for young machine-operators in the village.

Answers to the question "What are you most dissatisfied with in your work?" give an indication of the impact of the above-mentioned factors in creating some dissatisfaction (see Table 23).

The Table shows sufficiently clearly that the unevenness of seasonal work, high degree of exacting work, inadequate organisation and labour-payments are all serious problems.

Young machine-operators seem to regard seasonal work and the physical burden of farm work as the most acute problems. They are particularly serious, in so far as the state of equipment, repair and servicing are often at a low level. According to data from our investigations, the inadequacies of labour organisation include a shortage of machinery and spare parts (48 per cent of the young machine-operators cite this as the biggest problem), the low level of technology (16 per cent), insufficient material interest (16 per cent). Inasmuch as the beginner machine-operators express their greatest dissatisfaction here, it is important to do everything possible for them to start their labour activity with as much care and attention as possible from their older work-mates.

Farms have accumulated interesting experience in work with beginner machine-operators. For example, it has become a good tradition in mechanised teams operating the 'unspecified-duty' system to include a number of young machine-operators in the team. In the Millerov district of the Rostov region,

Table 23: "What are You Most Dissatisfied With in Your Work?" (%)

INDICATOR	AGE			
	17-19	20-23	24-26	27-29
Dissatisfied with earnings..................	18	12	11	8
Do not like the seasonal nature of the work......................	16	11	11	8
The work is too exacting..........	7	8	10	11
Those in charge are too rude, disrespectful and inconsiderate...	9	6	6	5
Work is monotonous................	10	8	4	4
No interest in farm work..........	3	2	2	-
Do not like the team.............	1	-	2	-
Poor relations with work-mates....	-	-	-	-

these teams have older comrades working alongside the young machine-operators. A quarter of each team, as a rule, is made up of machine-operators with less than a year's experience, the same proportion of those with between one and three years -- i.e., so that half the team needs assistance from more experienced fellow-workers. In our opinion, the mounting complexity of farm machinery and know-how makes it necessary to take account of this combination of junior and senior workers in forming Komsomol-youth work teams; this has the aim of seeing that the work schedules are met and of more effectively incorporating young people into the work. It is therefore important to ensure a certain independence of youth teams and, at the same time, to include experienced and skilled workers in them, persons capable of transmitting their experience to the youngsters by day-to-day contact.

The widespread system of tutorship is a laudable form of assistance to young machine-operators in mastering professional experience. A.V. Georgiev, First Secretary of the Altai Territorial Party Committee has explained the essence of this movement. He has said that today, when a farm worker equipped with knowledge and technical know-how is so vital, solicitude for his skill, his technical and productive culture, working and living conditions and spiritual well-being is becoming a matter of crucial importance. By doing everything necessary for the younger generation to tackle complex issues successfully, we are enhancing the prospects for higher production and the social welfare of the village. Tutorship is one way to resolve this problem[3]. It is distinguished by the friendly support and attention of the older generation for young men and women beginning their work career on collective and state farms. It transmits to them knowledge and experience, and a pride in belonging to the farming community. Thousands of veteran masters of their trade are now nurturing young people who will eventually take over from them. Every young machine-operator feels the benefit of this experience.

Stock-raising is a branch of agriculture that is in acute need of an influx of young people. At present, the proportion of output from public stock-raising on collective and state farms and other state enterprises is as follows: 83 per cent of the meat, 95 per cent of the milk, 85 per cent of the wool, 81 per cent of the eggs. The value of the gross farm output in 1970 was 86,992 million roubles, of which 42,862 million (approximately half) came from livestock[4]. By 1975, it is planned to increase the average annual meat output to 14,300,000 tonnes (dead weight), milk output to 92,300,000 tonnes, egg production to 46,700 million units, and wool output to 464,000 tonnes[5].

The Party regards an improvement in this area of prime importance, on which the population's welfare greatly depends. In his speech at the 24th Party Congress, L.I. Brezhnev made the point that "we are today confronted by the serious question in farming of how to make a further advance in livestock production" -- an area in which "we have to mobilise more fully all the reserves existing in collective and state farms"[6].

Young people are mostly interested in tackling production tasks that are connected with scientific and technological progress. Therefore, the more mechanised stock-raising becomes, the more young people will be attracted into it.

Sociological research shows that young stockmen are motivated in their choice of trade by the social significance of their work (38 per cent), by working in a socialist team and by good companionship (27.7 per cent), by an adequate level of material remuneration (18 per cent). By contrast with machine-operators, where the creative potential of work is a major consideration in the attractiveness of the job, few stockmen indicated this factor (only eight per cent of the young stockmen in the survey).

Young people are quite clear about those aspects of work in stock-raising that do not satisfy them: many labour operations, the physically exhausting and monotonous work that requires little skill or knowledge. That is why only a little over ten per cent of young people among the stockmen consider it necessary to improve their skill and continue studies so as to do better work.

It is noteworthy that only six per cent of the young stockmen link higher skill with higher earnings, while machine-operators put this indicator three and a half times higher. There is still an evident lack of differentiation in labour payment to stockmen according to skill, knowledge, experience, grading and work record. Due to recent government resolutions, the work record is now being taken into account. As one would expect, these measures, as the experience of the Lipetsk and Kirovograd regions and the Tartar Autonomous Republic reveals, are giving stockmen an interest in constantly improving their qualifications.

Many young people mention the awkward work regime in relation to studies and leisure-time as a factor having an adverse effect on attitudes to livestock work and to work-satisfaction. According to our calculations, the working time of young stockmen (on a weekly basis), while not exceeding eight hours a day, is unevenly distributed over a twenty-four hour period. This circumstance makes it difficult to combine work with study and is a major cause of the very low number of young stockmen who are actually studying. Our researches show that only a little over twenty per cent of stockmen have been transferred to double-shift work even at well-mechanised farms and places where they have every opportunity to transfer to progressive forms of labour organisation.

The need to change the work regime and create every facility for young stockmen to enjoy both engaging leisure-activities and studies has an objective basis. As stock-raising is being industrialised, the stockman's work today requires the constant addition of specialist knowledge and cannot, as hitherto, be confined to elementary work-habits and acquired experience. In expert opinion, the time has come for a really well-organised training of skilled manpower for work in stock-raising. This can scarcely be achieved by the efforts of collective and state farms alone. We need a well-founded state system of labour training in many trades for stockmen which would take account of the existing and future scientific and technical development in this area of farming. By their educational standards, young people are quite capable of acquiring up-to-date professional knowledge and they overwhelmingly express a desire for opportunities to continue their studies; they would clearly like to obtain the trade of a stockman whose work would be based on a new technological level.

There is still in farming a considerable amount of manual labour unconnected with any trade specialisation. As we have seen in looking at the structure of rural youth, a fairly large group of young people is engaged on manual work. Naturally, the group does not respond to stimuli to improve their knowledge and skill. Moreover, with the growth in professional experience and education, farm labourers tend to quit the job.

As mechanisation spreads throughout farming, farm labourers will gradually die out. Awareness of this trend in socialist conditions engenders in a labourer a contradictory attitude to work. On the one hand, he is a member of a socialist labour team and he appreciates the importance of and need for his work for the good of the community. A profound understanding of the social purpose of the work acts as the paramount motive in work-satisfaction. On the other hand, many labourers express their dissatisfaction with the nature of their work, describing it as primitive and monotonous, undemanding of any great creative effort. Therefore, many young labourers rarely feel their work requires them to improve their skill.

We have already noted that there are many persons in this group with secondary education; almost all of them wish to continue studies so as to change jobs in the future. The number actually continuing study (particularly up to 23 years of age) is fairly large -- as is to be expected. So there is bound to be a gradual withdrawal from unskilled labour and transfer to jobs demanding a higher standard of education and skill. It is consequently imperative for us to face the problem squarely of enabling young people to move out of unskilled and into specialised work.

As farming develops, the agricultural specialist is coming to play an increasingly responsible role. And this is where young people are coming to the fore. Today, virtually every other specialist on state and collective farms is under 30 years of age. If we consider that over 40,000 school-leavers come into agriculture as specialists every year, then we see that the share of young people is increasing in this group with every passing year.

Our researches reveal that young specialists assert quite unequivocably that they like the trade they have chosen (90 per cent of young specialists) and that their work is interesting (75 per cent). To questions concerning motives for selecting their specialism, many replied that they chose it because they were convinced of the interesting nature of the job. Half the people interviewed made the point that they had a fair prior knowledge of and faith in their future jobs. These judgements are bound to have a positive effect on work attitudes.

A creative attitude to the job is very much dependent on the extent to which the specialist systematically improves his knowledge and level of skill. Significantly, over half the young specialists are improving their skills; moreover, every sixth person is combining work with study in technical college or university. Only eight per cent of those interviewed expressed the opinion that they had completed their studies for good and needed no extra training.

While expressing their general satisfaction with their work, young specialists pose a number of questions that have to be resolved for them to work better. Many said they were unhappy about work organisation, about having to waste so much time on unskilled jobs. They claim that often the best part of their time has to be spent on matters related to material and technological supplies, marketing products, filling in forms and information sheets, settling all manner of trivial issues.

Statistics from a time-study of a working day among 818 specialists, conducted by the Krasnodar Regional Agricultural Board, are eloquent testimony of the amount of time-wasted. They show, for example, that collective-farm chairman and state-farm managers spend about a third of their time outside the farms -- in district centres or on journeys connected with material and technical supplies; as much as 76 per cent of the time was spent on meetings and conferences. Similarly, the working time of farm specialists is often spent irrationally. Agronomists spend, for example, ten-twelve per cent of their working time travelling from one field to another, from one team to another, and a further fifteen per cent on compiling documentation and accounts. Many young specialists complain of their lack of knowledge of economies and management, psychology, ethics and aesthetics, and scientific labour organisation. This goes some way to explain the fact that young specialists more readily agree to work as branch or sector experts than as brigadiers or farm managers, or even to take on responsibility for a relatively small labour team.

Although only a small number of specialists are unhappy with living conditions (as many as 80 per cent have been less than three years in the job), we must focus attention on this figure because one in every two people is thinking of giving up his job for this very reason. It is the duty of every team, as happens in most collective and state farms, to do everything possible to make the first (most difficult) years of a young person's working life as interesting as possible.

Young specialists also indicate other difficulties: the uncertain nature of the jobs they have to do, the pettiness of the supervisor or, on the contrary, the lack of attention or help from managerial personnel.

All these issues worry young specialists, mainly because they wish to work 'at full throttle', to enhance their growing responsibility as technologists and farm managers; they rightly believe that their specialist training and working conditions should enable them to develop their best qualities.

Lenin's words about the need to value and cherish specialists as "the greatest attainment of technology and culture without whom there can be no such thing as communism" are as valid as ever, since the requirements for knowledge and culture have grown as never before. The agricultural specialist today receives general recognition thanks to his creative endeavour embodied in the attainments of human knowledge and technical progress.

2. Socialist emulation

Socialist emulation occupies a special place in the promotion of the work and social activity of young people, their political and civic maturity. It has the vital function of attracting young people into administering production, of shaping a new attitude to work and using the highest forms of its organisation, and in enriching man with new social relations. As Lenin once put it, socialist emulation raises Soviet workers "to a level of work in which they can manifest themselves, develop their talents and bring out their skills..."[7]

Of the 93 million trade unionists in the USSR today, some 74 million are taking part in socialist emulation; over half of the are engaged in the movement for a communist attitude to work[8].

The scope of socialist emulation in the countryside is enormous; every category of young people is involved in it. While 50 per cent of young people had been involved in socialist emulation on the eve of the last war, as many as 65.6 per cent were involved in 1946, 78.0 per cent in 1957, 86.8 per cent in 1966, and 91.7 per cent in 1971[9]. On 1st January, 1971, over 13 million trade unionists were engaged in socialist emulation in farming.

The high standards of skill, shock work, enterprise and selfless toil are all powerful sources of labour and social activity among rural youth; they considerably enhance the part young people play in social production. It is hardly surprising that young men and women should take a favourable attitude towards both the economic and moral importance of emulation. From our surveys, we found that some 80 per cent of young farmers mentioned emulation as developing a sense of responsibility, evincing a desire to work better, to come out on top; it was also said to bind people together, strengthen discipline, help people to master skills faster and to promost mutual assistance and comradeship.

At the same time, young people indicate vast unutilised reserves for organising emulation better and increasing efficiency. They say, for example, that there are deficiencies in selecting and determining specific emulation indicators, weak information on progress in fulfilling obligations, insufficient involvement of all participants in deciding upon and adopting particular pledges. They refer specifically to a correct application of Lenin's principles of organising socialist emulation.

CHAPTER FOUR

SOCIAL AND POLITICAL ACTIVITY

Social and political activity is becoming the norm among all working people in socialist society. It is the greatest attainment of socialism and its historic advantage over capitalism that it should involve the common people in running society. To be involved actively in public affairs means helping to construct the new society, breaking free of the narrow confines of private life, making people active participants in all socio-economic and cultural changes and giving people a real sense of being masters of their own country.

Numerous factors testify to the extent of activity and mounting interest of rural youth in socially-useful matters, particularly the expenditure of non-working time on this sphere of activity. According to surveys carried out by V.G. Mordkovich, each young village worker spent an average of 4.1 hours each month in 1966 on social and political activity. Our own researches, undertaken by the Moscow University Laboratory in 1971, reveal that this expenditure had increased to 6.4 hours. This time-expenditure is even more encouraging if we compare it with that surveyed in the early 1920's. Time-budget studies made in 1922 and 1923 show that a young workingman spent only 0.27 hours, and a young woman worker 0.3 hours, a month on social activity. Young peasants devoted even less time to such activities. While the major portion of time spent on social work in the 1920's went on attending meetings, and only ten per cent directly on social work in organisations, today the ratio of active to passive social work has altered radically. The performance of individual or collective tasks for public organisations nowadays accounts for over 80 per cent of such time expenditure[1]. The mass political activity of rural youth is evident, too, in the growing interest in social and political world and home news. Thus, 33 per cent of our sample attended lectures on socio-political themes in 1966, and 48.1 per cent did so in 1971. The enormous interest of young people in socio-political information is apparent from newspaper circulation. Virtually every young villager now reads a daily newspaper

(90 per cent). When questioned further, the respondents disclosed that they were particularly interested in home news (56 per cent), village news (48 per cent) and world politics (54 per cent). Two out of every ten keep abreast of socio-political news through specialised literature.

Nearly half young people, according to our survey findings, are now involved in some form of social activity in the village. Of these, some twenty per cent receive regular assignments, the rest carry out various commissions for public organisations 'now and again'.

The nature of socio-political activity is extremely varied. Thus, 30 per cent of young men and women with regular assignments are involved in agitational and propaganda work, 23.5 per cent take part in electoral Party/*Komsomol* work, eight per cent are engaged in public self-administration in the village (in *druzhiny*, comradely courts, parents' councils, etc.), 8.5 per cent are in public administration and control bodies at work.

There are no forms of public activity today in which young people do not play their full part. Young collective and state farmers work as deputies to local Soviets, take part in the work of standing commissions and act as *Komsomol* and Party activists. With the active assistance of young farmers, public principles of administration are beginning to develop through public inspection, brigade, farm, club, library and parents' councils; the young people are active in the *druzhiny* and the *Komsomol* Spotlight groups.

As L.I. Brezhnev made clear in his speech at the recent All-Union Student Rally, this type of community work develops the best features of a Soviet person, "a person with strong moral fibre". It helps to encourage wonderful workmen "full of enthusiasm, selfless endeavour and interest in their labours", who combine a lofty Party-mindedness with efficient work[2].

It is important to note that young villagers from all walks of life are being drawn into this multiform social activity (See Table 24). The data show that half the assignments of a socio-political nature are being undertaken by young people engaged directly in material production and doing predominantly manual labour. This reveals the overriding trend in socialist society for developing the creative socio-political activity of the vast mass of the working people.

Another marked feature is the greater activity of skilled young machinists over other occupational groups. If we compare the public activity of machine-operators with young labourers, we see that the share of machine-operators is much higher in all social assignments.

Table 24: Distribution of Permanent Public Assignments among Young People in Different Occupational Groups (%)

OCCUPATIONAL GROUP	Agitation and Propaganda	Party and Komsomol Work	Trade-Union Work	Self Administration Activities (Druzhiny, Comradely Courts, etc)	Cultural and Educational Work	Public Administration and Control Work on The Job	Sports Work, DOSAAF*	Work on Councils and Commissions
Managerial personnel and specialists.....	53	40	57	28	50	10	32	32
Employees...........	21	20	18	12	6	15	9	11
Machine operators...	6	15	6	16	25	19	29	22
Technical servicers..	2	5	2	16	25	19	29	22
Constructors.........	1	2	4	3	10	5	5	-
Stockmen.............	6	6	-	3	-	19	-	20
Non-mechanised labourers............	3	3	-	5	-	15	10	4
Labourers without a speciality.........	6	4	7	10	3	2	5	3

DOSAAF (Voluntary Society of Soviet Army, Air Force and Navy) is the Soviet civil defence organisation.

N.B. The percentages given in the table were calculated separately for each type of social assignment.

Apart from the permanent public assignments, young men and women in the village (approximately every fourth person) takes part in occasional public assignments which do carry considerable social and educative weight. Of all public assignments, we mention here only a few that have become widely popular among rural youth. These include taking part in electoral campaigns and undertakings of a socio-political nature (meetings, conferences, etc.); arranging subscriptions to journals and popularising newspapers, magazines and popular literature among rural residents; popularising new festivals and celebrations and forming new traditions; nature preservation and local history work; participation in subbotniki and voskresniki; helping to improve village amenities; campaigning for higher cultural and hygienic standards (introduction of public sanitation and hygiene); assisting the village school to improve its facilities and to give schoolchildren a good communist education.

The nature of occasional public assignments reveals their significance in strengthening the ties between young people and community goals, in uniting rural youth around socially important tasks and in developing a collective psychology.

Analysis of the motives for social and political activity shows that rural youth associate it primarily with the overall goals of improving economic, cultural and social standards in the Soviet village and implementing the decisions of the 24th Party Congress. Thus, to the question "What encourages you to do community work?", the following answers were given:

"The striving to combat shortcomings and actively to improve living and working conditions" -- 30 per cent; "A desire constantly to be part of the life of my collective, to be at the centre of events in my work" -- 22 per cent; "A desire to improve the work of the Komsomol organisation" -- 22 per cent; "An awareness of the importance of fighting for justice and young people's rights" -- 19 per cent; "An appreciation of the importance of my assignments and the need for social work" -- 10 per cent; "Personal aims and an urge to get on, to ensure promotion in my job" -- 4 per cent.

As these results indicate, the motivation of young people is linked with social and political ends that emanate from the overall interests and tasks of socialist construction. Only one in every twenty-six replies mentioned motives outside the sphere of public interest.

A socially-aware, creative attitude to community action does not arise, in Lenin's words, "out of thin air"; it grows out of living conditions, of purposive organisational and educative work in combating a psychology alien to socialism. The participation of young villagers in social and political affairs is indissolubly linked with the activity of rural public organisations. It is precisely these cells that unite young farmers. The Party and Komsomol organisations, local Soviets, trade union and other public organisations are the major inspirers of socio-political activity. In recent years, they have greatly stepped up their work in promoting the initiative and independence of young people. Of all the persons in our survey, 34 per cent noted serious positive changes in the work of public organisations and greater opportunities for young people to excel for the benefit of the community in general.

Young Communists and Komsomol members are indeed the most active section of rural youth. This is apparent from data on distribution of social assignments (see Table 25) by Party membership.

Table 25: Distribution of Social Assignments Among Party and Non-Party Members

PARTY STATUS	NATURE OF ASSIGNMENT		
	Permanent Assignment	Occasional Assignment	No Assignment
Party members or probationary members	51	34	15
Komsomol members	27	35	38
Non-Party members	8	14	78

Party and Komsomol members are engaged on average four times more often than others in community work; 85 per cent of young rural communists and 62 per cent of Komsomol-members have assignments. The community work they do is particularly important. Young Party and Komsomol members account for 80 per cent of all young farmers engaged in public self-administration (on councils, work administration bodies, village management boards, etc.)

Being a Party or Komsomol member puts a high responsibility on each person for his particular team and requires him to show an example of "the application of communist principles in practice". This is what determines the vanguard role assigned by communists and Komsomol members to promoting the community activities of all young people in the village.

Social and political activity greatly depends on the nature of work and occupational qualifications. Table 26 shows that the highest percentage of those doing community work is to be found among managerial personnal and specialists (80 per cent); then come rural industrial workers, those servicing machinery and machine-operators. Here the percentage of those with assignments amounts respectively to 44, 42 and 38. A lower degree of engagement in community work among young farmers is observed among those doing non-mechanised jobs (32 per cent) and those engaged in construction and stock-raising (30 per cent).

The lowest involvement is among non-specialists: only one in four carries out such assignments. It is worth recalling that this group also had the lowest educational level and was least satisfied with the work.

A certain trend is observable also in the type of assignments performed. Thus, young managers, specialists and employees carry out 75 per cent of the assignments related to mass agitational work (lectures, propaganda, agitation), political education (leaders of circles, seminars, political-education cabinets, etc.), amateur artistic activities and the work of club and library councils.

Educational standards naturally influence the social activity of rural youth; knowledge gives greater opportunity to carry out functions concerned with socially-useful work. The results of our investigation show that persons possessing secondary and special secondary education tend, *ceteris paribus*

Table 26: Distribution of Social Assignments by Occupational Group (%)

OCCUPATIONAL GROUP	Nature of Community Work	
	Permanent Assignment	Occasional Assignment
Managers and specialists	46	34
Machine-operators	18	25
Persons servicing machinery	10	36
Constructors	9	21
Stockmen	10	20
Persons doing non-mechanised work	7	25
Non-specialists	7	17
Industrial workers in the village	16	28

(occupation, free time, etc.) to be involved in community work two or three times more often than workers with only 4-6 classes of education. On the whole, young men and women with secondary or higher education perform 56.5 per cent of all social assignments.

The findings of sociological surveys reveal that young men and women engage equally in social and political activity; there appear to be no fundamental differences in regard to the content and character of the work being done. Thus, of the sample survey among those permanently performing social assignments, girls and women make up 52 per cent, men -- 48 per cent. On the other hand, 47 per cent of those engaged on their chosen community work are women and 53 per cent men. This situation demonstrates the de facto equality of men and women both in material production and in the social life of the Soviet village.

According to all our surveys of collective and state farms, girls and young women display no less a degree of interest in public affairs than men. In fact, the ratio is slightly higher for women among employees and stockmen in the 16-23 age group.

But opportunities for active participation in public affairs markedly diminish with age, family and household responsibility, and work on the private allotment. While unmarreid and married women without children or with only one child share social assignments with men, the gap widens two- or three-fold as soon as the second child appears. More than half (57 per cent) of the young women not participating in social work are those with two children who, for various reasons, do not leave their children in nurseries (sometimes because the villages lack nursery facilities). This situation exists, with slight fluctuations, in all occupational groups.

The correlation of community activity and age indicates that the greatest involvement occurs in the first and second age groups (16-19 and 20-23). A relative fall takes place in the latter groups (24-26 and 27-30); with women this decline appears even in the second age group. Thus there is a clear link between the declining involvement in social activity and the increase in household work, the existence of two or more children and the growing amount of non-working time devoted to work on the private allotment.

The overall tendency towards an improvement in material welfare, culture and living conditions in the village are, of course, changing the status of farm workers, particularly women. Already today in farms with good communal services and adequate supplies (due to efficient collective and state farm work), the age-group differences in social activity are neglible. For example, the Komsomolets Collective Farm in the Alexandrov district of Stavropol territory now has several modern cultural and educational institutions, largely by virtue of improved farm production and the developing social principles within the collective; as a consequence, the farm enjoys a mass involvement of young people of all age groups in community activity[3].

Our analysis enables us to draw the basic conclusions that young villagers today are overwhelmingly active in social and political affairs; they regard this work as important and necessary -- as is clear from their attitudes to social assignments (See Table 27).

Table 27: Attitudes to Social Assignments

GROUP	CONTENT OF REPLIES			
	Carry out any assignment freely, realising the importance of social work	Indicate responsibility to the organisation giving the assignment	Carry out assignment unwillingly because consider it useless	Try to refuse assignments; do them under pressure
Managers and specialists	55	37	-	-
Machine Operators	31	29	2	1
Persons Servicing Machinery	18	31	2	2
Constructors	27	20	2	-
Stockmen	24	20	2	-
Persons Doing Non-Mechanised Work	25	25	3	-
Non-specialists	24	22	2	-

The Table shows that young people carry out social assignments of their own free will, with inner conviction and responsibility. Only three per cent of the number in the survey believe community work to be of little use or value. Follow-up investigations of young people's social activity, undertaken by us in 1971 on farms of the Kaluga and Rostov regions, Stavropol and Krasnodar territories, confirm these earlier findings. The great bulk of young people (82 per cent) with social assignments expressed satisfaction with the nature of their assignments and emphasised their significance for the success of the common cause and for their own development. A mere one out of every thirty persons in the survey was dissatisfied with the assignments that he or she had to undertake ("the assignment was not to my liking").

Stable attitudes in regard to social and political activity and an eagerness to take an active part in community affairs are typical not only of those undertaking assignments; many young people classified as "passive" speak expressly of their desire to engage in community work (35 per cent of persons in that group made this clear). The chief reason for their non-participation was because "We wished to do this work but there was nobody to suggest or arrange it". There is therefore a big reserve and area of activity for the primary Komsomol branches to work on in the village.

The contribution of young farmers to running collective affairs and their participation in social and political life are accorded wide public recognition. Citations of moral encouragement have been given to 28 per cent of those who have taken part in the social life of their collectives and have carried out assignments of public organisations. More than half of these have received honorary diplomas and valuable gifts. Many young people have received public thanks for their efforts.

Social and political activity, as revealed in analysis of the nature of social activity, and the lofty recognition of its importance, is an essential feature of the social portrait of village youth.

The involvement of young people in social and political activity is becoming increasingly important today when the Party is demanding that every Soviet person "should feel himself a citizen in the full sense of the word, interested in community affairs and bearing his full share of responsibility for them[4]", should display the maximum initiative in running public affairs and the country. It is a prime task today to involve all groups of rural youth, every girl and boy, in active social and political work, with an awareness of the qualities that here unfold. This is the direction in which the Leninist Komsomol is developing its work.

CHAPTER FIVE

MORAL OUTLOOK OF RURAL YOUTH

1. Communist philosophy as the basis of the moral outlook of Soviet youth

Youth is a time when character is formed, plans are made, a philosophy of life and a moral outlook take shape. By taking an active part in strenghtening and improving socialist farming, in the social and political life of the country, and in promoting cultural and communal standards and facilities in the village, rural youth thereby act as class-conscious participants in the building of a new society. They comprehend the purpose of life and their place within it, they associate their personal ideals with the great goals of the people.

The traits that distinguish the moral outlook of a young person in the land of the Soviets include ideological resolution, political tempering, unbounded loyalty to the teaching of Lenin and the cause of the Communist Party.

The Leninist Komsomol sees its task in teaching all young men and women creatively to master Marxist-Leninist theory, to form a materialist outlook, to develop ideological conviction and to take a class approach to social phenomena[1].

Philosophy manifest itself in the way people think and act, in the whole character of their activity. Most important of all, it is manifest in their civic responsibility -- their sense of personal responsibility for what is going on around them, their ability to stand up for their ideals, to approach all phenomena and events from class positions and with the interests of the people uppermost.

Our rural youth exhibit a high degree of civic responsibility, profound optimism, a striving to be useful to the people and to the homeland, collectivism and patriotism. A question we put to over 5,000 young people was:

"Indicate the qualities you think most praiseworthy in your contemporaries". The overwhelming majority of replies (90 per cent) gave preference to such qualities as a striving to be of use to the community, an ability to work well, honesty and justice, kindness and modesty, mutual assistance and comradeship. Young people value these virtues and manifest them in their daily life and practical work. The results we obtained in numerous interviews with managerial and administrative personnal of farms and production-teams show that most young people (over 80 per cent) perform their assigned work conscientiously, with an awareness of the common goals. Virtually all administrative personnel emphasise the positive attitudes of young people, their thirst for knowledge and their attraction to all that is new and progressive.

Young people wish to see their villages well-appointed, with a high level of culture. They express concern over incidents of drunkenness and hooliganism and they take an energetic part in combating them. They are deeply interested in prospects for further economic development in collective and state farms. This is evident from answers to the question "What issues most concern young people?" (as a percentage of people in the survey): "Cultural development of the village" -- 56 per cent; "Combating drunkenness and hooliganism" -- 40 per cent; "Higher living standards for villagers" -- 26 per cent; "Farm development" -- 19 per cent; and "Campaign against embezzlement of public property" -- 15 per cent.

A public confidence, an understanding of real prospects that open up extensive opportunities to young people, and direct participation in their implementation enrich young people spiritually, fill their lives with a profound and multifaceted meaning, and create a sense of satisfaction with their own personal lives. When we asked "Are you content with the way your life has turned out?", we received the following replies (as a percentage of the number surveyed): "Content" -- 56 per cent; "Not completely content" -- 31 per cent; and "Discontent" -- 9 per cent.

Despite the difficulties and deficiencies prevalent in the modern village, young people are totally optimistic in their evaluation of the way their lives are being shaped. This satisfaction cannot be put down to complacency or smugness. They link their optimism and satisfaction above all with the possibility of becoming involved in common work, in concerted action to improve the economy, culture and communal amenities in the countryside, in a clear awareness of communist ideals.

Young people show an appreciation of the experience and sacrifice of the older generation. They see and understand the enormous role and selflessness of the older generation in winning and upholding the new life. It is therefore quite natural that more than 90 per cent of those questioned have a high opinion of the relationships between young people and their older comrades. This brings out the respect of young people for the views and ideals of the older generation, an appreciation of their care and assistance in everyday work and personal lives. When we asked rural youth what favourable influence the older generation has on them, we received the following replies: "Older people are eager to impart their work experience" -- 79 per cent; "They transmit proper attitudes to life" -- 75 per cent; "They point out incorrect behaviour" -- 73 per cent; and "They help us to resolve vitally important problems" -- 84 per cent.

The older generation represents tradition and experience, knowledge and valuable habits, which are transmitted to youngsters through education and training. On the other hand, the older generation is also represented by the real people with whom a young person comes into contact. The family, school, work-team -- these are the specific social milieux in which the older generation's influence is most felt on the confuct of young people and their chosen paths in life. In their answers, young people make the point that their mothers (42 per cent) have most influence on them in regard to behaviour and their chosen career; fathers come second (27 per cent), favourite school-teachers come next (17 per cent), then older work-fellows or the work-team as a whole (15 per cent).

Our survey confirmed that the youth display most interest in active forms of study, in discussion, question-and-answer evenings, and conferences. Interest in lectures on the international situation is immense.

Political study enables young people more profoundly to master ideological principles, to understand the principal laws of social life, it equips them with a knowledge of the class approach to social phenomena. Ideological work, as young people themselves mention, exciets an interest in problems and events in international and home affairs. Suffice it to say that in excess of 90 per cent of rural youth read newspapers daily, and more than half show a constand interest in material on life and events in our country and on events abroad. Overall, every third young villager is engaged in a form of study within the political enlightenment network.

In their work, deeds and conduct, young people exhibit a firm bond with communist principles and moral standards. This is reflected in their plans and value-orientations.

2. Plans and value-orientations of rural youth

As the culture and living standards of the Soviet village improve, as the content and form of peasant work-organisation alter, so the plans of young people differ from one generation to the next. It is therefore of interest to compare results of social surveys made at different periods of Soviet history.

What constituted the personal ideals and aspirations? How have the plans of rural youth changed over the years? To answer these questions, we compared social research of the 1920's with that undertaken between 1967 and 1970 in the same regions.

During the 1920's, the well-known Soviet rural researcher, A.M. Bolshakov, carried out wide-ranging surveys into the living and working conditions of peasants in the former Tver Province (nowadays the Kalinin region). He published his findings in Derevnya 1917-1928 gg. (The Village 1917-1928). His results show conclusively that the new social circumstances had a decisive effect on the way young people chose their future jobs. Typical of those years was the desire to take up new types of work, new trades that were lightening and changing the peasant's labour.

Young people in the village realised with increasing clarity that the primitive, onerous work of the tiller of the soil, the elementary forms of farming produced miserable results in every respect. The responses revealed the constant refrain that "using grandfather's methods will not improve farming", "will not help others" and "will not earn much".

Some 40 per cent of people in the survey who linked their fate with farming mentioned new aspirations, such as the following: "I want to be a skilled farmer", "an agronomist", "a technician of farm machinery", etc. Young people thereby exceeded the confines of the age-old attitudes to life and labour in the countryside.

Other young people dreamed of gaining a trade directly connected with the village, but requiring a high educational level (teacher, doctor, engineer). In selecting such a career, they indicated their "importance to the village" and the high prestige they enjoyed.

Meanwhile, many schoolchildren were taking up a craft of an individual nature (blacksmith, tailor, cobbler) which would ensure, they felt, a reasonably high living standard in the village at that time.

Among motives for selecting a job in the 1920's, community importance and opportunities came high on the list. There was a stated desire for the future job "to lighten the burden of the peasant", "to be of assistance to others", "to contribute towards becoming a man of wide knowledge" and "to be useful to the Soviet state".

It is natural that at a time of small commodity-production and the survival of market relations in the countryside, an important motivation in choosing a job should be "high earnings" (37 per cent), "work that guarantees an easy and carefree life", and so on.

A few young people even remained captive to ideas that their chosen profession should not only gain them "an easy life" and "big money", but also afford them the opportunity to "do nothing", live at the expense of others. Such "professions" as horse-dealer (2.4 per cent), landowner (0.9 per cent), speculator (0.9 per cent) and mistress of the manor (0.9 per cent) were all included.

When asked whom they took as a model on which to shape their lives, young people indicated fundamental changes in value-orientations and plans by comparison with pre-revolutionary years. They expressed their ideals in terms of people who selflessly gave their work and knowledge for reconstructing village life and farming. They were attracted by such virtues as hard work, a good knowledge of the job, solicitude, kindness and sensitivity in regard to others. The most popular examples for emulation were Bolshevik revolutionaries, particularly Vladimir Lenin. They saw in them the embodiment of their own personal ideals.

All these findings show that even in the 1920's the basic outline of rural youth in the new society was taking shape. They were firmly associating the prospects for their own personal lives with the overall well-being of their homeland, the Soviet state.

Our young contemporaries answered the same questions in the same regions in 1968; in all we questioned 861 persons in the 8-18 age range. The results reveal that the ideals and value-orientations of the 1960's very much reflect far-reaching social changes in the USSR, scientific and technical progress and the education of the younger generation in the revolutionary, labour and militant traditions of the Soviet people.

The range of professional interests had broadened immensely, and the diapason of choice of future jobs had expanded. While a total of 21 professions had been named in 1926, it had increased to more than 70 in 1968. Moreover, most of these were at a high level of complexity; some, like construction-engineer, geologist, electrician, radio-operator, chemist, pilot, were virtually unheard-of by villagers in the 1920's, although, nowadays, it is not unusual or unrealistic to aspire to become any one of them.

Of the total number of people in the survey, nineteen per cent directly relate their future work to farming; all of them want to become machine-operators and acquire a mastery of technical and similar intricate work. Only a tiny number wish to do jobs that do not need a high degree of skill.

Today's rural youth associate their plans and values with active participation in all branches of the economy. This is fairly obviously expressed in the motives given for selecting a future trade. As in the 1920's, though with more forceful argumentation, they link the job with its creative and purposeful opportunities that present conditions conducive to their own development.

Material considerations, work purely for high earnings -- a fairly prominent feature of the 1920's -- are now of less importance. Thus, there had been a certain, though small, parasitical tendency among rural youth of the 1920's; this is now totally absent. But, as earlier, the social significance of the chosen profession is a principal motive for the younger generation of the late 1960's. This motivation is, however, now expressed more profoundly, filled with a new meaning. It is distinguished by a well-substantiated choice of profession through education, the rapidly growing flow of information and, most importantly, the accumulated experience of building a new life.

This aspiration for socially-useful activity is clearly expressed in the ideals of the younger generation. They associate these largely with people who have given their lives for freedom and independence of their homeland. Over 66 per cent of those questioned name as their ideal a personality of the October Revolution or a hero of the Civic or Great Patriotic wars. As before, Lenin is the most obvious model whom all young people wish to emulate and on whom they form their vital plans. Other attractive figures include innovators in production, heroes of the five-year plans and merited workers of their own particular farms.

The investigations showed that the generations of the 1920's and 1960's linked their lives with the overall aims of socialist society both in choosing a job and in selecting a personal example on which to model their lives. Other social surveys of recent years[2] would tend to indicate the same tendencies.

In studying the plans of young people, it is important to clarify what motives they are guided by in choosing their future jobs. Among replies to the question "Why did you choose your job?", the highest percentage (27) said "It is my vocation, I have dreamed of that job". In regard to personal preference, other replies were roughly as follows: "I like the village and farming, and this determined my choice" -- 15 per cent; "Though I am not keen on the work, I know it is very necessary" -- 13 per cent; "I chose the work on the advice of my parents or near relatives" -- 10 per cent; "I was allotted this work after my studies" -- 8 per cent; "The work is well paid" -- 4 per cent; "The work is easy and clean, and this determined my choice" -- 2 per cent.

The answers indicate that most young farm workers do follow their vocation, do work that is necessary, and that these are the guiding principles in their orientation on agricultural work.

The results also testify that every fourth per son regards his work as temporary, related to the lack of any other choice. This opinion reflects the difficulties that exist in the village for young people to realise their ambitions, largely because there is still a great mass of unskilled and unattractive manual labour to be done. This opinion tells us that a large section of young people engaged in farming is ill aware of the opportunities that agriculture today offers.

Young people's evaluation of various aspects of their work is of importance in revealing value-orientations in regard to work. They highlight socio-economic conditions typical of socialist production. In answer to a question about what attracts them in work, they cite such items as the socialist work-team, its solidarity, the importance and significance of farm output for the country, work-relations of companionship and mutual support, etc.

The distribution of answers to the question "Do you like the team in which you work?" was as follows: "I like my work-team" -- 23 per cent; "I have an interesting job" -- 21 per cent; "I like farming and the chance to work in the open air" -- 19 per cent; "I like the importance of farm production" -- 15 per cent; "The work demands initiative and discipline" -- 14 per cent; "Good, friendly relations with my comrades" -- 10 per cent; "The fairly high earnings" -- 9 per cent; "The work is not too tiring" -- 7 per cent; "The solicitude of those in charge" -- 5 per cent.

These judgements show conclusively that socialist labour includes a whole set of values both functional and socio-economic. Socialist work as a basic value of life reveals in its functional content such value-elements as creativity, inventiveness, rationalisation and improvements in labour organisation. They express the objective tendency for social labour in socialist conditions.

The socio-economic form of work includes the following values: companionship, mutual assistance and socialist emulation. It is therefore hardly surprising that young people can express satisfaction with their work even when it is unattractive and limited in its creative potential. Over 80 per cent of rural youth in our investigation (who expressed a positive evaluation) substantiated their satisfaction by reference to the values of socialist work.

Another important value-orientation of rural youth is their firm belief in education. When we studied the plans and values of rural school-leavers, we found that 90 per cent of them intended either to study full time or to combine work with study. Similar findings have come from a survey of school-children in the Orlov region[3].

Nearly half the young rural workers (48 per cent) expressed a desire to continue studies. Of these, 32 per cent intended to study in agricultural college, 21 per cent in school, 19 per cent in a technical college, 12 per cent in medical college, 10 per cent in a college of education, and 6 per cent in schools of cultural enlightenment. So we see that many young people connect a higher education with the application of knowledge to some form of farm-activity.

Value-orientations in regard to education are fairly stable in all socio-demographic groups. But the number of people studying full time and particularly those combining work and study is by no means the same in all professional groups. This is apparent from two occupational groups of rural youth -- machine-operators and non-specialists (see Table 28).

The Table shows that far more machine-operators are studying than non-specialists. Even greater differences are observable if we compare the latter with specialists, among whom one in every three is combining work with training.

It is interesting that both machine-operators and non-specialists under 19 have practically identical educational aspirations. Here we see the effect of the school in shaping their outlook. But, as they grow older, other features of everyday life and work come into play, and their educational aspirations diverge. The share of machine-operators studying at ordinary school diminishes, while the number in specialised schools and colleges increases. On the other hand, non-specialists in that age range show a sharp drop in educational aspirations all round.

Table 28: Rural Youth Combining Work and Study (%)

OCCUPATION	AGE	EDUCATIONAL INSTITUTION				
		Agricul-tural	Technical	Humanit-arian	Secondary School	Trade School
Machine-Operators	17-19	2	2	-	24	8
	20-23	8	8	1	8	5
	24-26	2	-	1	6	2
	27-30	4	1	-	4	-
Non-specialists	17-19	3	1	-	25	5
	20-23	3	-	-	6	-
	24-26	4	2	2	-	-
	27-30	1	-	-	1	-

When we bear in mind that the bulk of non-specialists is fairly great and is a constant reserve for supplementing skilled workers, it is clear that the task facing the Komsomol is urgent is these young people are to be persuaded to continue their education. This is all the more important in that the prospects for farming involve an intensive transformation of peasant labour through science. The turbulent process of labour-change in agriculture into a form of industrial work is already demanding highly-trained and educated experts.

We have noted that young people in the Soviet village display a reasonably high degree of social and political activity. This is understandable, in so far as the environment of universal labour and social activity, the socialist moral and political climate involves young people from an early age in the personal participation of everyone in public life; it stimulates a need for active participation in all the affairs of one's group and of society as a whole.

The striving of young people to be useful to their country, the ability to fight for the ideals of communism is an attainment of victorious socialism. Conscious participation in the country's social and political affairs has become a major value of socialist youth. They associate their plans with the mastery of this value, seeing in it the necessary means of affirming themselves as socially-significant beings.

Socialist labour, educational improvement and the mass character of social and political activity have all enhanced the orientation of rural youth towards the values of spiritual culture. This orientation is manifest both in the desire for education and in the profound interest in books, the cinema, theatre, music and amateur artistic activity. Over half the people in our survey mentioned reading as their favourite activity. Books have become the trusty companions of young people in the village. It is hard to find a house in the modern village which has no books or which does not subscribe to a newspaper or magazine.

More than half the young people indicated that they had a home-library which contained both fiction, specialised literature and socio-political books. True, the number of books in such personal libraries is still not very large: only 3 per cent of the survey claimed to have more than 100 books; a further 10 per cent said they had between 20 and 100, and 32 per cent had up to 20 books. Yet there is no disputing the trend towards an increasing number of books at home. This process could be even more rapid is the book trade, the distribution and propaganda of books in the countryside, corresponded to the present demand and needs of villagers. One in three young people in our survey expressed a desire for more classical and modern literature, for technical, agricultural and medical handbooks, for more varied and eye-catching advertising of new books.

The families of young farm workers normally have a radio and many have television sets. Moreover, the differences in radio and TV-set ownership are very small among the families of different youth groups.

The favourable opportunities for young people to reinforce and improve their orientation on cultural values are obviously associated with a rise in their material welfare. The research carried out in recent years confirms that, as a factor for evaluating work satisfaction, earnings normally take second place to such motives as the social significance of work and the creative opportunities[4]. Even though earnings do not play an all-consuming part, they are nevertheless an essential ingredient in value-orientations in regard to work. Young people regard them above all as a necessary condition for their cultural development. This attitude is apparent in answers to the question "If you had spare cash, what would you spend it on?". Most youngsters said they would spend it on touring, trips to the city, buying a motorbike or car or other items necessary for diversifying their activities.

Rural youth indicates two basic sources of material well-being. Apart from payments for work in the public farm-sector, they still value highly earnings from subsidiary farming. According to the results of our investigation, only 15 per cent of those in our survey do not have a subsidiary farm. Over 70 per cent have orchards, 56 per cent own cows on their farms, 67 per cent poultry, 41 per cent pigs, and 31 per cent sheep and goats. Young people show a certain uniformity in their attitudes towards this (see Table 29). Thus, in reply to the question "What prevents you from leaving the village for the town?" many people answered that they did not want to leave their private plots. This is evident in all groups, although the older age groups are more represented (31 per cent).

At the same time, the results show another tendency -- for reducing and even abolishing the subsidiary farming. This is to be expected, in that a large share of work on the private plot is done by women. And this work, our investigations show, takes up between seven and fifteen hours a week, depending on the number of employed family-members. With the rise in material living conditions from the collective-farm sector, people are now realising how wasteful it is to keep up a private subsidiary farm. Private farming is decreasing every year on collective and state farms. It is, for example, no longer necessary to keep cows on private allotments of the Zhdanov Collective Farm in Gyulkevich districk (Krasnodar territory) because for several years the farmers have had all their dairy produce needs met. They now have no privately-owned cows at all and they have therefore cut down the size of their subsidiary farms around their orchards. Such examples are numerous. But it would be wrong to force the pace of this process. "The time will come," D.S. Polyansky has said, "when collective farming will reach a level at which the collective farmers themselves will turn away from subsidiary farms as economically unprofitable and unnecessary. But to abolish them unjustifiably, to accelerate the process now artifically would be to ignore the facts of life in the village."[5]

The plans and value-orientations of rural youth are increasingly being realised directly in rural conditions. This is clear from the fact that almost half of those in the survey were firm in their intention of staying put in the village. When asked "Do you wish to leave for the town?", 29 per cent were in favour, 44 per cent against and 23 per cent did not know.

Rural life itself is an important value for young people, constituting an essential element of their desire to live and work in their native village. During our investigation, we asked the following question: "What attracts you to life in the village?" The reaponses were as follows: "I love nature" -- 35 per cent; "My relatives and friends live here" -- 31 per cent; "I like village life"-- 26 per cent; "I like my job" -- 25 per cent; "It is easier to live well in the countryside" -- 16 per cent; "I like farming" -- 14 per cent.

At the same time, the search for opportunities to realise personal plans may well take young people away from the villages. They do not always see their future in farming or the village because they link their plans with the town. The essential differences between town and country are, after all, factors that cannot be ignored. The town is the centre of industrial work and advanced culture and therefore remains a big source of attraction. It is in the town that young people believe it possible more quickly and better to realise their aspirations for skilled labour, for continuing their studies, for acquiring cultural and spiritual values and for better living conditions.

We may examine the attitude of young people to the town in Table 30.

The results testify to the fact that the orientation on the town is more or less the same for all groups. The dominant motives include the chance of continuing studies, receiving a good trade, and spending free time in a cultured and interesting way. Material conditions and earnings do not take such an overriding place as they did a few years ago.

Nowadays, young people strive to obtain knowledge and a trade and to have extensive access to the wealth of human culture. These changes in value-orientations, which are reflected in the motives for migration, are backed up by other sociological studies. Thus, V.I. Staroverov reports that the major motivation for rural migration up to 1965 was the desire to improve material conditions and obtain higher and more stable earnings. Between 1953 and 1957, this motivation amounted to 46.6 per cent; in the period 1958-62 -- 35.6 per cent; 1963-65 -- up to 30.4 per cent, remaining the largest single consideration. But by 1966-67, its share was down to 19.5 per cent and on a level with such motives as a desire to continue studies (16.8 per cent), improve working conditions (15.2 per cent), and to get a trade (14.3 per cent). In the last two years (1968-69), the material-welfare motive gave way to all these other motives and amounted to only 11.7 per cent. According to our findings, this index is even lower for rural youth in all age groups and amounts to no more than five per cent.

The investigation of plans and values shows that rural youth are putting more store by those aspects of life which require active and creative participation in socially-useful activity both in work and in social, cultural and political affairs. This tendency is manifest in the striving of young people to find more creative work, to acquire a wide variety of knowledge and more fully to master spiritual and cultural values. This process is an expression of the overriding law-governed development of socialist society -- the formation of the spiritual outlook of a new person with an all-round developed personality.

Table 29: Attitudes of Rural Youth to Private Subsidiary Farming (%)

Youth group	Maintain present size	Reduce size	Abolish it
All youth groups	33	9	9
Specialists			
Men (17-23)	47	11	18
Men (24-26)	59	16	5
Men (27-30)	45	18	17
Women (17-19)	41	18	18
Women (20-23)	30	10	27
Women (24-27)	44	14	14
Women (27-30)	37	28	12
Machine-operators			
Men (17-19)	48	14	7
Men (20-23)	54	9	13
Men (24-26)	61	6	6
Men (27-30)	57	7	8
Stockmen			
Women (up to 19)	58	9	6
Women (20-23)	60	9	9
Women (24-26)	82	5	4
Women (27-30)	50	6	5
Men (up to 26)	53	5	15
Men (27-30)	70	17	-
Non-specialists			
Men (up to 19)	60	12	7
Men (20-23)	60	6	3
Men (24-26)	55	6	-
Men (27-30)	46	2	5
Women (up to 19)	58	9	9
Women (20-23)	54	7	1
Women (24-26)	61	1	5
Women (27-30)	54	15	4
Managerial personnel	56	17	7
Housewives	47	4	13

Table 30: Attitudes of Rural Youth to Town Life (%)

Youth group	What attracts you to the town?				
	Chance to continue studies	Possibility of spending time more culturally and interestingly	Living conditions	Permanent work, grading	Material conditions
All youth groups	39	30	21	13	5
Specialists					
Men (up to 25)	47	33	22	11	5
Men (24-26)	31	35	29	7	1
Men (27-30)	23	44	29	21	4
Women (17-19)	50	54	15	7	7
Women (20-23)	37	58	20	6	2
Women (24-26)	34	60	29	16	4
Machine-operators					
Men (up to 19)	34	35	11	10	3
Men (20-25)	44	39	23	13	1
Men (24-26)	31	36	23	17	4
Men (27-30)	15	32	22	13	5
Stockmen					
Women (up to 19)	49	38	14	10	7
Women (20-23)	28	40	18	9	2
Women (24-26)	14	35	10	12	1
Women (27-30)	10	41	24	17	7
Men (up to 26)	20	38	10	15	7
Men (27-30)	11	29	26	11	6
Non-specialists					
Men (up to 19)	37	45	12	9	-
Men (20-23)	46	37	15	15	6
Men (24-26)	15	55	23	11	4
Men (27-30)	16	30	28	9	14
Women (up to 19)	14	27	16	9	11
Women (20-23)	28	37	22	13	7
Women (24-26)	21	36	25	23	8
Women (27-30)	10	36	20	17	11
Managerial personnel	21	36	20	17	1
Housewives	27	27	18	15	4

CHAPTER SIX

LEISURE ACTIVITIES

1. Facilities for enjoying leisure in the village

The desire of young people for more creative activity is not confined to work; it embraces all aspects of life.

Free time or leisure plays an important part in shaping the lives of young people. Leisure is an activity that takes place in free time and is determined by a person's independent choice in each sepearat case. The effective participation of a young person in labour and community affairs greatly depends on the content, orientation and nature of this activity. Marx once wrote that "free time is both a time for leisure and a time for doing higher things; of course, it turns the person enjoying it into another subject, and as another subject, he enters into the direct process of production"[1]. Leisure and work, consequently, are closely intermeshed. Activity which a person carries on in his spare time, as Marx pointed out, is a paramount means of making him an all-round developed person. It can be used for acquiring spiritual and cultural values, developing ability and talent, inculcating aesthetic, physical and moral qualities in the human personality.

It is not unusual to hear the opinion that leisure is a purely personal affair, that people's spare time may be spent freely at their own discretion. Of course, every person uses free time as he wishes. But that does not mean that leisure, as a sphere of personal life, lies outside the influence of society. Leisure is a social phenomenon and performs certain social roles.

Every social system creates a social content of leisure corresponding to that system. As an essential part of social life, leisure performs certain functions of production and reproduction of a particular historical nature. In an exploiting society, the ruling classes always try to keep the content of leisure within the confines of the standards and requirements necessary for maintaining and strengthening their rule.

The life of the pre-revolutionary peasant was burdened with onerous toil and subject to poverty. At the end of his daily and weekly work, virtually no time remained for leisure. What spare time did remain went on activities that suited the autocracy. The tsarist authorities and the Church saw to it that the muzhik did not spread his interests beyond the 'pub', the church and the home.

The Revolution liberated the peasant masses from economic and spiritual tyranny and made them the masters of their own destinies. The complicated job of transforming the old patriarchal way of life affected not only economic relations and the political system; it deeply penetrated the entire everyday life and leisure of the peasant. The cultural revolution in the village radically changed the whole character of rural leisure, filling it with fresh spiritual interests and cultural needs having a socialist content. This is evident in the findings of social researchers in the early Soviet years[2].

In subsequent years, there is discernible a further strengthening of a socialist tendency in using free time. Thus, working men spent 2.6 times more time on social activities in 1930 than they had done in 1923, while working women spent 5.6 times more, and housewives -- 2.7 times more[3]. During these years, the great mass of the peasants hankered after knowledge and culture.

The state did all it could to provide facilities: it built schools, opened reading rooms and libraries, set up hygiene-and-sanitation points and other amenities that helped to change the everyday life and culture of the village.

While villages had a total of 11,300 libraries with some 4,400,000 books and magazines in 1913, by 1922 the book fund had almost trebled to 11,400,000 and in 1928, there were 20,900 libraries with 25,400,000 book and magazine items[4].

The increase in village clubs was even more rapid. Throughout the whole of the Russian Empire, there had been no more than a hundred village clubs in 1913, yet there were 8,600 in 1922 and as many as 30,000 by 1928[5].

All subsequent peaceful years of socialist and communist construction saw a further increase in provision of cultural amenities in the village. By 1971, villages had a total of 90,700 libraries with a book fund of 588,100,000 copies, and 115,900 clubs with a staff of almost 3,500,000[6].

The fundamental transformation in the social and economic basis of life in the countryside and the implementation of Lenin's cooperative plan brought about a new status of the peasant in production and in the whole system of social relations. To build socialism in the countryside, however, it was necessary to overcome the age-old force of habit of the petty proprietor, the parochialness of such views on life. During this momentous campaign by the Party, the peasant became "an active participant in collective labour and social life"[7].

A new socialist way of life and new traditions took shape in the course of the acute struggle against the old way of life, conservative traditions, mores and prejudices. A socialist production-collective took the place of scattered peasant-strip farming. From the outset, the labour collective became the centre of all life in the countryside, having a decisive influence on all areas of activity of the farm worker. Collective principles of life and work began to permeate the entire life of the peasant, including his leisure activities. The development of the collective-farm movement greatly reinforced socialist tendencies in the use of free time.

The Leninist *Komsomol* has paid constant attention to the leisure of rural youth. Back in December, 1934, a resolution of the *Komsomol* Plenary Meeting "On the Mass Cultural Work of the VLKSM, mainly in the Village" emphasised the need to create every possible facility for socialist collective forms of leisure for young villagers. The resolution called upon *Komsomol* organisations to take responsibility and show every concern for the work of every club, every library, 'red corner' and sports-ground, "regularly to arrange youth evenings, open-air entertainment, especially during festivals, to introduce new songs, games and dances, also to hold poetry readings, exhibitions and displays of artistic work, group viewing of films, etc." The Plenary Meeting also made special provision for the training of personnel to launch this far-reaching programme.

Facilities for spending leisure in a group certainly did not mean that individuality was being pushed into the background. On the contrary, thanks to the socialist collective, greater activity of the personality and wealth of its individuality became a definite value, a basic criterion for real success in the work of organising and enjoying leisure in the countryside. Vigorous participation in organising new forms of leisure enriched a young person's personality and gave shape to socialist virtues.

Today, leisure activities are being transformed through economic attainments and the economic success of collective and state farms; the Party is guiding leisure-activity in accordance with the overall goals and tasks of building communism.

The most salient feature of changes in leisure-facilities in the contemporary village is the growing amount of time available for leisure. This increase depends on more industrialisation of farming and specialisation. The use of new forms of labour organisation, the shift-system and a more even employment over the year all help to make the work regimes more orderly and to release a certain portion of time for leisure.

Meanwhile, free time also increases through fundamental changes in living conditions and everyday life. As the Party Plenary Meeting held in July 1970 noted, "a vigorous process is underway in the countryside for housing, cultural and amenities construction...Overall consumption of electricity in the countryside has risen by 59 per cent; some 3,496,000 apartments have been provided with gas -- by comparison with only 616,000 with gas four years previously. We have extended the network of clubs, cinemas, libraries and consumer amenities. Radio and television are becoming permanent features of village homes."[8] An even more extensive programme of cultural measures is being carried out during the Ninth Five-Year Plan (1971-75). These changes are lightening the burden of housework and affecting the structure of time expenditure, leaving an increasing proportion for leisure. Much depends here on improvements to provision of services. The sphere of services, organisation of working people's leisure and recreation are not simply sectors earmarked for plan-fulfillment, but services directly concerning human beings with a wide variety of tastes and human feelings.

According to the USSR Central Statistical Board, the total services in the countryside more than trebled during the previous Seven-Year Plan (while they only doubled for the country as a whole). In one year along (1967) the total services increased 18 per cent for the country as a whole and 28 per cent for the countryside[9].

The amount of time-expenditure of villagers in recent years provides some idea of the improving services and the structural changes in agricultural work. According to surveys made by A.S. Duchal between 1962 and 1964, men had an average of 20.37 hours free time during the summer, or 12.1 per cent of their weekly time-budget; the corresponding figures for women were 7.8 hours and 4.7 per cent[10]. Time-budget studies among rural youth, carried out by N. Ryabov in 1966-67, revealed that weekly free time among men was 25.37 hours, or 15.01 per cent, and among women 10.87 hours, or 8.6 per cent[11]. Our time-budget studies among young machine-operators (in the summer of 1970) show that weekly free time amounted to 25 hours, or 15 per cent.

One of the most marked characteristics of present-day village life is the development of the services sphere. The massive reconstruction of rural life and culture are being reinforced by the wide scope of building both of modern residential dwellings and of entire complexes of cultural amenities. It is today hard to find a single village or farm where this great and complex task has not been tackled.

The main element of leisure is <u>man</u> himself and his requirements, his demands and interests which require corresponding means for their satisfaction. To ensure the optimal conditions for leisure presupposes a certain coincidence of people's requirements and abilities with the means for realising them. Therefore, any change in the content of requirements and abilities inevitably evinces changes in the means of enjoying leisure. And, vice versa, the creation of new means of leisure presupposes corresponding requirements from people.

Despite the rapid cultural construction and successful economic development in the present-day village, the potential and requirements of young people often surpass the production and cultural conditions in which these requirements are realised. This contradiction, if it is not taken into consideration and if practical measures are not taken to deal with it, harbours the danger of turning young people away from the village.

When we asked "What village problems most concern young people today?", most young people (56 per cent) said that the main one was lack of cultural facilities, of any variety in provision of leisure or entertainment. This cultural deficiency is largely a result of poor housing facilities (26 per cent), lack of clubs (eight per cent), shortage of sports-amenities (23 per cent), poor work by clubs and houses of culture (38 per cent). It is interesting to note that many young people are demanding more money from farm managements for cultural and educational needs and sport. It is obviously important to involve young people in transforming the cultural profile of a village, to create fresh spiritual values.

While displaying concern for the leisure of young people, we should bear in mind both their rapidly growing requirements and the lack of desire among some of them to fill their leisure with any socially-useful content; some wish to spend their spare time on useless pursuits and some come under the influence of religious prejudices. Here there is an enormous area for the Komsomol to work upon; its efforts can greatly enhance the educative power of the collective, can create a social and psychological climate in which young people's efforts would be directed towards a socially-useful and creative use of leisure-time, so that they obtained satisfaction and enjoyed life to the full. The Sixteenth Komsomol Congress drew attention to the need to create every possible condition for "improving the organisation of young people's leisure", for the use of free time to broaden young people's political and cultural outlook, their scientific, technical and artistic knowledge and creativity, their community work and physical development[12].

2. Leisure activities

Rural youth today spend their leisure in a great variety of ways, both collective and individual. They watch TV and do unpaid voluntary work in their spare time, they read and engage in mass festivities, attend sports spectacles and go in for sport, have parties and engage in literary disputes, visit a club or carry out social assignments, do amateur art activities and enjoy many other forms of leisure. Apart from analysing individual forms of free-time use, we also tried to establish the role and functions of group forms of leisure among rural youth. The figures in Table 31 show the extent of their development, revealing the most widespread forms of mass leisure. It would seem that the following activities are of permanent concern to young people; festivals devoted to labour and revolutionary events, meetings with famous people, evenings of entertainment, amateur art activities, sporting contests and many other collective forms of leisure. Here young people have the opportunity to display their many talents and satisfy requirements for extensive community with their peers through joint participation in socially-useful work.

Table 31: Collective Forms of Leisure in the Village

Mass leisure-forms	Regularly	Irregularly	Not at all
Harvest festivals	65	15	10
Lectures, talks, discussions	28	39	17
Evenings of entertainment	23	36	32
Voluntary, unpaid labour	21	54	24
Sports contests	20	27	31
Meetings with famous people	19	40	34

Evidently, young people put a premium on collective leisure forms. Harvest festivals enjoy particular popularity; they are not only held universally, but they are conspicuous for the great wealth of forms they take and national traditions. This celebration of work, the crowning of the farming year, reveals a fresh attitude of rural workers to group activity, it enhances the role and significance of socialist labour, and respect for the farmer's trade. Young people consider this festival especially important because the fruits of long and selfless labour by many people embody also their own knowledge and experience, the first successes and failures, the difficulties of mastering their profession. Tamara Sikorova, Komsomol secretary on the Komsomolets Collective Farm has said that "our Harvest Festival is a most colourful celebration. We can see clearly all that we have achieved during the year. The tables and diagrams show the rise in production-indices by the year. The best brigadiers are awarded Red banners, and the leading workers have their names inscribed in the Book of Honour and are given the title 'Merited Collective Farmer' and 'Master of the Golden Hands'. The festival is one of enormous enjoyment and merriment. It is also a good school for us, the young people."

Being a display of achievements and a family occasion, the Harvest Festival fortifies labour solidarity and demonstrates the measure of participation of each person in gathering the fruits of the farming year -- i.e., the harvest. To the minds of young people, this festival always excites profound sentiments, engenders fresh aspirations and plans. In the words of many farm managers in the Millerov District of the Rostov Region, the harvest festivals focus attention on the sum total of work of the primary collectives and help substantially to reinforce the self-supporting labour-organisation system whereby payment is made for the final produce; this has become a major factor in the campaign for production efficiency.

Unfortunatley, harvest festivals are still not held everywhere on a regular basis; as young people remark, they are not held at all on some farms. The rural Komsomol certainly has enough power to see that this form of leisure becomes a bright decoration of village life, that it should embody the best traditions, creativity and vigour of youth.

Evenings of entertainment are widespread in the village. This form of leisure can involve young people in many forms of independent activity either as participant or organiser. We have many rural clubs and palaces of culture where evenings of entertainment are real festive occasions and help to uncover new talent and gifts. Where young people show their initiative and ingenuity, take part in drawing up programmes, they will certainly never suffer from boredom or be passive onlookers.

Nonetheless, the best examples of cultural leisure have still, sad to say, not become nation-wide. When we asked what cultural measures were most necessary for rural youth today, we were told mainly discussions, interesting conferences and quizzes (27.5 per cent), good and interesting evenings of entertainment (25.5 per cent), better club work with adequate amenities (20 per cent).

Voluntary unpaid labour on Saturdays and Sundays has in recent years been given regularly both in the country and the town. This remarkable collective form of popular participation in joint work during free time combines both productive labour and leisure. Selfless and voluntary group labour in 'work-festivals' has particular attraction for young people.

One may justifiably ask what leisure is it if, in effect, it is replaced by work? Undoubtedly, such 'voskresniki' involve socially-useful work; but the important point is that the work is carried out in free time. Collective productive work here becomes a means of spending one's leisure-time. Moreover, the combination of work and leisure most forceably expresses the socialist trend of its development. By taking part in voskresniki, young people are selflessly helping to improve their villages, cultural amenities and farm work.

Sport comes high on the list of popular attractions for young people in the village. Their leisure is increasingly being enriched by the construction of sports-grounds and stadiums, the setting up of matches in various sports. Well-organised sport brings young people together, gives them an interest in the affairs of their work-teams. T.P. Cherkasov, Chairman of the Nasha Rodina Collective Farm, has rightly said that the sports complex his farm built a few years ago has repaid itself many times over. Many farm workers have taken up a sport, thus cutting down sickness. It is now a favourite activity to visit the 'little sports town'. The athletics, football, volleyball, boxing and several other sections have over 150 members each.

In spite of the obvious value of sport as an attractive and socially-useful form of leisure, its development in the countryside is still greatly lagging behind the demand for it among young people. More than half the young people (53 per cent) revealed that they never do any sport, and virtually a third (31 per cent) noted that no sports facilities exist in their villages.

It is noteworthy that the level of activity in regard to sport, in all occupational groups, is more or less identical, with the exception of stockmen (see Table 32).

Table 32: Participation in Sport among Rural Youth by Occupational Group (%)

Occupational group	Regularly	Occasionally	Not at all
Managerial and administrative personnel	14	30	50
Specialists	12	26	51
Machine-operators	13.8	32.5	46
Stockmen	6.5	12	72
Non-specialist manual labourers	12	25	55.5

Coincidence of data on distribution means equal conditions and opportunities for all villagers to take part in the given form of activity during their leisure-time.

The measures taken by the Party and the Komsomol aimed at satisfying the requirements of young people and of society for all-round developed people will undoubtedly, in the nearest future, tell on the development of mass sport in the village and enable us considerably to increase the number of people who regularly pursue a sport.

Thousands of young men and women have begun to take their tests in the new "Ready for Labour and Defence" fitness programme, introduced in March 1972. Displays and examinations in physical training and military sports are becoming a test of the skill and strength of young men about to do their military service. More and more frequently, rural youths are coming into the armed forces with their sports-badges and even rankings. The bulk of young people between 17 and 23 cite sport as a particularly desirable and attractive pursuit among the various forms of leisure; they say that more sports-grounds, stadiums, ice-skating rinks and so on should be built in the villages. They themselves are quite prepared to give up part of their free time to help construct these amenities.

Meetings with famous personalities are becoming an increasingly popular form of group leisure. Follow-up surveys in the same locations have shown that in the last three years alone the number of such encounters have nearly doubled. This is a direct result of the extensive propaganda and organisational work of the Komsomol. Well-known in Altai Territory, for example, are the names of prominent corn-growers, Heroes of Socialist Labour Mikhail Golikov and Pyotr Chechevitsa, Brigadier of the First Girls Tractor Brigade in Altai (Varvara Bakholdina), leading workers (Yakov Tyazhin, Ivan Popov and many others). They are all frequent guests of young people and each has something of value to impart.

Pyotr Chechevitsa, for example, is a leading machine-operator on the Tselinny State Farm in the Volchikhinsky District, a man who possesses several agricultural trades. A former worker at the Moscow Voikov factory and a virgin-lands pioneer, he has trained scores of able machine-operators. Local communists chose him to be a delegate to the 24th Party Congress and he was made Hero of Socialist Labour for his excellent work.

Ivan Popov is a corn-grower at the 'Fiftieth Anniversary of the Komsomol' State Farm in Rebrikhinsky District and a communist. It is as a result of his paternal care that many girls of the farm have acquired a machine-operating skill and that the girls' machine-operating detachment led by Nina Grigorieva was adjudged to be the best women's brigade on 1970 results.

Varvara Bakholdina was one of the first woman machine-operators in the country and is a Cavalier of the Order of Lenin. She is now responsible for successful women's machine-operating brigades in Shipunov District.

Naturally, encounters with such personalities help to promote new traditions and habits in the village, assist young people to adopt the values of socialist society, to form their own plans in life.

Some of the really mass, traditional leisure-forms on many farms include the following: "Spring is Coming", "The Harvest Calls", "The First Furrow Festival" and "The Russian Silver-Birch Festival". They give a send-off, as it were, to the new harvest, "give their blessing" to farm workers for their noble work.

While stressing the significance of young people's collective leisure-forms, however, we should not forget individual leisure. A correct understanding of the essence of collective leisure-forms, their place and importance in the free-time structure helps us more profoundly to appreciate the role of individual forms. Moreover, only a unity of collective and individual leisure forms can correspond to requirements for the harmonious and all-round development of the human personality.

Every person has certain personal inclinations and interests. One person takes pleasure in sitting over a book, another is a keen music buff, yet another collects stamps. One person likes company, another prefers solitude. Attention to individual leisure-forms can enrich the personality and make it more interesting and colourful.

The results of several surveys in recent years show a considerable expansion in the range of spiritual requirements and interests of rural youth[13]. It is quite common for them nowadays to enjoy pastimes that exert their mental faculties. This is clear from replies to the question "How do you prefer to spend your free time?" (See Table 33).

Table 33: Free Time Use by Rural Youth (%)

Reading books, newspapers and magazines	71
Watching TV and listening to the radio	56
Going to the club (cinema, dance)	48
Meeting friends	27
Nature-rambles	16
Games (cards, dominoes, lotto)	16
Playing musical instruments	6
Passive leisure	2

We see that a marked feature of today's rural youth is its penchant for reading -- which is more popular than any other form of individual leisure. We obtained a similar picture when we asked a parallel question: "How would you spend your free time if you had more of it?" Once again first preference went to reading. In the first instance, reading gained 51 per cent and in the second 37 per cent. After that, from the first study, follow studying (36 per cent), watching films (31 per cent), housework and family affairs (29 per cent), sport (19 per cent) and meetings with friends (16 per cent).

Our findings show that reading retains its top place among all forms of cultural leisure in every occupational group in absolute terms, though not relatively. This factor is marked in analysing statistics on various groups reading books during a year, by age, sex and trade (see Table 34).

The table shows that the highest percentage of people reading over ten books a year is to be found among specialists (who have highest educational level in the village), while the smallest interest in books is among unskilled manual labourers -- only 45 per cent of whom had read more than ten books in one year.

While noting the overall high degree of interest among rural youth in reading books and journals, let us look more closely at <u>what</u> they actually read. The questions we asked were "What articles do you read most?" (see Table 35).

The findings show that a large sector of young people reads literature about love and friendship, and the heroism of Soviet people during the revolution, Civil and Patriotic wars. This theme is popular for all occupational and demographic groups. Themes of science-fiction and adventure are also popular among young people, irrespective of age. Interest in social and political literature is more in evidence among managers and specialists, and among communists and <u>Komsomol</u> members.

Listening to the radio and watching television occupy a prominent place in young people's leisure. Our findings give a clear picture of the extent of popularity of these forms of leisure (see Table 36).

Table 35: Favourite Reading Matter Among Rural Youth

Literature (books)	%	Newspaper material	%
Love and friendship	52	Life and events in our country	56
Heroes of the revolution, Civil and Patriotic wars	47	Foreign events	54
		News about rural life	48
Adventure, science-fiction	22	Satire	27
Production and technical literature	21	Moral and educational subjects	26
Social and political literature	8	Scientific and technical news	25
		Sport	22
		Komsomol affairs	21

Table 36: Frequency of TV and Radio Use Among Rural Youth

INDICATOR	Listening to the radio			Watching Television		
	Daily	Occasionally	Not at all	Regularly	Occasionally	Not at all
Distribution of answers (as a % of those questioned)	82	14	4	48	37	15

Rural youth are particularly fond of the radio because of its easy accessibility and variety of programmes. In all groups they give preference among

radio programmes to the news, the "Youth" and the "Land and People" programmes, concerts and plays. Among intellectuals and high-skilled workers, interest rises in programmes about innovations in the field of science and technology, and commentaries on international affairs.

Young people enjoy broadcasts on local radio stations about exemplary personalities in the locality, advanced experience, work successes in emulation-campaigns, and concerts by local amateur groups.

Findings on the favourite TV programme of young girls and boys in the village are shown in Table 37.

Young people's interest in TV programmes is not confined to watching films. Many young viewers also enjoy such artistic and mind-testing TV programmes as quizzes, documentary films, "Horizon" (49 per cent) and TV spectacles (38 per cent).

There is a mounting interest among both collective- and state-farm youth in intellectual programmes: television news -- 18 per cent, information on science and technology -- 13 per cent, educational programmes -- six per cent. They display a lively interest in political information both on radio and on television.

Films hold a special place among cultural leisure-forms in that they reflect many aspects of life, help young people to comprehend the momentous changes taking place in our country. Films about the present day, on patriotic, moral and everyday themes seem to be most popular. When we asked how often young people went to the cinema (as a percentage of those questioned), we received the following answers: "Once a week"-- 51 per cent; "2-3 times a month" -- 21 per cent; "Once every 1-2 months" -- 17 per cent; "Not at all" -- 8 per cent.

While taking note of the stable interest in films, we should also bear in mind the many appeals to improve film-performances in the village. Village clubs are said frequently to show films that are old or poor, and this is justly criticised by young villagers.

Visits to relatives and friends is still a traditional way of spending leisure time among villagers. In fact, they devote much of their spare time to this, mainly on week-ends or holidays[14]. According to several time-budget studies, time expended on this leisure-activity among young people amounts to about one sixth of free time -- i.e., 2-3 times less than among older people.

Traditions and habits that have taken root are most apparent precisely in this form of leisure; hospitality and cordiality, the permanence of direct community of village people, concern for relatives, and other positive factors. Such traditions are constantly being enriched by the experience of socialist relationships in the countryside and the practice of collective work. It is not only kinship relations that are today influencing this leisure form. Fellowship relations at work are increasingly becoming decisive also in the choice of friends in one's spare time and in enjoying holidays and family occasions together.

As V.N. Pervitsky writes: "We love these get-togethers; this is how we get to know more about the lives of each of our companions. And we take pride in the fact that they live in a cultured way, have all they need and respect their friends. Relatives are even sometimes hurt that we do not spend enough time with them; simply we have become accustomed to one another. And we are happy and used to sharing everything -- our joys and woes, work and play."

But, unfortunately, there is another side to this form of leisure. Visits to relatives and friends are not infrequently accompanied by drinking parties and such empty games as cards, dominoes and lotto.

The specific characteristics fo each leisure-form and its share in the free-time structure demand constant attention both to the present and to the future. Of course, no administrative methods or devices must be used in dealing with this situation. The basic force of influence must be education, particularly public opinion, which can be a unique regulator of human conduct in everyday affairs.

Our study of the conditions, content and form of leisure reveals that the construction of socialism and communism in our country has radically changed the leisure of young people. Affirmation of the socialist way of life has engendered new trends in the content and form of leisure; it is an important factor in shaping the spiritual world of young people and in involving them in independent life -- precisely because it is socially significant, it presupposes a multitude of spiritual and cultural values, wide-scale independent initiative and the increasing extension of collective forms of leisure. That is why it is the most important sphere of activity for Komsomol organisations. In emphasising the importance of leisure in the communist socialisation of the younger generation, the 24th Party Congress noted the need to enable all boys and girls to use their free time sensibly so as to expand their political and cultural horizons and to possess harmoniously-developed personalities.

Table 37: Favourite TV Programmes Among Various Occupational Groups, by Sex and Age

Nature of work	Sex	Age	Films	Spectacles	News	Science and technology	Educational programmes	Sport	"Round table" discussions	Quizzes, "Horizon", etc.
Specialists with secondary special and higher education	M	17-23	47	25	16	22	8	27	5	41
		24-26	51	27	16	29	6	38	16	37
		27-30	56	35	30	24	8	52	15	48
	F	17-19	62	43	15	13	7	20	9	60
		20-23	63	47	12	14	10	25	14	59
		24-30	66	52	34	25	9	25	21	66
Machine-operators	M	17-19	62	25	12	16	5	47	5	44
		20-23	57	20	13	16	3	39	15	42
		24-26	58	27	18	23	6	39	15	38
		27-30	62	36	26	21	7	37	8	40
Stockmen	F	14-19	59	32	8	6	2	17	4	41
		20-23	54	32	11	11	3	6	5	36
		24-26	60	42	10	4	2	7	7	45
		27-30	60	50	16	3	1	11	5	45
	M	14-26	56	15	12	-	-	23	10	35
		27-30	55	32	17	11	5	20	8	29
Roster-workers (po naryadam)	M	14-19	57	21	8	28	3	38	2	35
		20-23	75	46	31	21	3	59	9	59
		24-26	46	33	8	11	-	22	8	24
		27-30	59	43	22	15	7	36	14	43
	F	14-19	54	36	9	3	1	13	1	34
		22-23	52	28	9	3	7	15	9	28
		24-26	55	58	13	10	6	8	6	38
		27-30	63	61	23	5	3	12	12	52
Managers	-	-	62	37	26	28	13	37	18	53
Industrial workers	-	-	72	56	14	14	7	33	8	63
Workers servicing farm-machinery	-	-	52	13	9	13	4	36	11	40
Constructors	-	-	57	25	12	12	1	32	11	43
Housewives	-	-	56	45	15	13	4	9	3	29

CONCLUSIONS

Young people are playing a prominent part in the building of communism. There is no sector of construction in socialist society where the younger generation has not demonstrated vigorous creative initiative. Alongside the older generation, Soviet young people are tackling common tasks and participating in the fight to realise the communist ideal.

The training and involvement of the younger generation in active work and socio-political activity are ensured by the consistent observance of Marxist-Leninist principles of work with youth, and by Party and Komsomol guidance of communist education.

This study of youth in the Soviet village has revealed a number of typical features of their social profile. We have seen their energy in work and community affairs, their civic responsibility and initiative, collectivism and loyalty to communist ideals, their optimism and social conviction, the steadily rising level of education and professional training, the wide horizons and multiplicity of interests. All these facets of the social profile of rural youth are the results of fundamental change in social and economic conditions, greater culture in the village, and the direct participation of the youth themselves in bringing about this transformation.

The social qualities of youth are being strengthened and improved through scientific and technological progress and the resolution of erstwhile intractible problems of farm production; they are bringing about higher standards of culture and everyday life in the Soviet village.

The high standards of education and the nature of the training of rural youth for life give them every opportunity to acquire intricate technical skills and a variety of expertise, energetically to take part in social and political activity. They are in the forefront of the campaign to intensify farm production, to introduce modern science and technology and advanced experience into all branches of farming. Moreover, they are actively engaging in many community affairs.

The virtues of rural youth are manifest in their ideology, value-orientations and vital plans, which are conspicuous for a striving to be useful to people, to make a contribution to the common cause in the fight for communism. For them, communism is a real prospect, the raison d'etre of life and the rationale of their activity.

Rural youth is a complex, widely-differentiated social and demographic group in Soviet society. This differentiation stems from the division of labour in agriculture, the essential differences in the work being done by socio-occupational groups. A marked dependence exists between the nature and conditions of work, the forms of its organisation, the extent of work-satisfaction, and the attitudes of young people to farming. That is why it is so important to take cognisance of the work of each separate occupational group.

People in the modern village are doing all they can to make young people's lives stimulating and their work creative, to improve education and professional skill, to expand and enrich cultural services and to raise cultural standards. The lives of young people and their effective contribution to the common cause greatly depend on the successful implementation of these tasks.

Today, rural youth and their organiser, the Leninist Komsomol, are bending their efforts, together with all Soviet people, to implement the agricultural programme outlined at the 24th Party Congress. The social features of rural youth that have taken shape during the Soviet years are becoming increasingly manifest in their variegated activity in further transforming all aspects of life in the Soviet village.

NOTES

Introduction

1 L.I. Brezhnev, Leninskim kursom, Moscow, 1970, Vol. 2, p. 98.
2 Materialy XXIV s'yezda KPSS, Moscow, 1971, p. 300.
3 Ibid.
4 Ibid.
5 Ibid., pp. 79-80.

Chapter 1 Rural Youth as an Object of Sociological Research

1 V.I. Lenin, Collected Works (Russian), Vol. 7, p. 343.
2 See V.I. Lenin, "Internatsional molodyozhi," Collected Works (Russian), Vol. 30, pp. 225-229; "Krizis men'shevizma," Vol. 14, p. 163; "Zadachi revolyutsionnoi molodyozhi," Vol. 7, pp. 341-356; "Zadachi soyuzov molodyozhi," Vol. 41, pp. 298-318.
3 V.I. Lenin, Collected Works (Russian), Vol. 30, p. 226.
4 See G. Schelsky, Die Skeptische Generation, Minich, 1965.
5 C.A. Reich, The Greening of America, New York, 1970, p. 187. (this quotation is not to be found on the page indicated -- or elsewhere in the book).
6 See Pravda, 24 March, 1972.
7 See H. Marcuse, One Dimensional Man. Studies in the Ideology of Advanced Industrial Society, New York, 1964.
8 Materialy XX1V s'yezda KPSS, p. 75.
9 Materialy XV1 s'yezda VLKSM, Moscow, 1970, pp. 19-29.
10 L.I. Brezhnev, Leninskim kursom, Vol. 2, p. 262.
11 See VLKSM ot s'yezda k s'yezdu, Moscow, 1970, p. 41.
12 Narodnoye khozyaistvo SSSR v 1970 godu, Moscow, p. 404.
13 Ibid., p. 412
14 Migratsiya sel'skovo naseleniya: tseli, zadachi i metody regulirovaniya, Novosibirsk, 1969, p. 78.

Chapter 2 Working and Living Conditions in the Countryside

1 V.I. Lenin, Collected Works (Russian), Vol. 37, p. 358.

2 Torzhestvo Leninskovo kooperativnovo plana. Materialy Tret'yevo Vsesoyuznovo s'yezda kolkhoznikov, November, 1969, Moscow, 1969, pp. 4-5.

3 See Materialy XX1V s'yezda KPSS, p. 39.

4 Ibid., pp. 47-48.

5 See Narodnoye khozyaistvo SSSR v 1970 godu, p. 374.

6 Strana Sovetov za 50 let, Moscow, 1967, pp. 152-153; Narodnoye khozyaistvo SSSR v 1968 godu, Moscow, 1969, p. 413; Narodnoye khozyaistvo SSSR v 1970 godu, p. 372.

7 See Narodnoye khozyaistvo SSSR v 1970 godu, p. 372.

8 Yu.S. Meleschenko, Chelovek, obshchestvo i tekhnika, Leningrad, 1964, p. 96.

9 See V.I. Lenin, Collected Works (Russian), Vol. 5, pp. 138-139.

10 Ibid., Vol. 42, p. 187.

11 Strana Sovetov za 50 let, p. 154; Narodnoye khozyaistvo SSSR v 1968 godu, p. 419; Narodnoye khozyaistvo SSSR v 1969, Moscow, 1970, p. 393; Narodnoye khozyaistvo SSSR v 1970 godu, pp. 378-380.

12 See Materialy XX1V s'yezda KPSS, p. 156.

13 See Sel'skaya zhizn', 7 August, 1970.

14 See V.I. Lenin, Collected Works (Russian), Vol. 35, p. 67.

15 See Materialy XX1V s'yezda KPSS, pp. 264-265.

16 See A. Dushkin, "Effektivnost' nauchno-tekhnicheskovo progressa," Ekonomika sel'skovo khozyaistva, 1971, No. 5, p. 22.

17 Materialy XV1 s'yezda VLKSM, p. 10.

18 Strana Sovetov za 50 let, pp. 242-243.

19 Narodnoye khozyaistvo SSSR v 1970 godu, p. 519.

20 Narodnoye khozyaistvo SSSR v 1969 godu, p. 560; Narodnoye khozyaistvo SSSR v 1970 godu, p. 537.

21 Narodnoye khozyaistvo SSSR v 1970 godu, p. 529.

22 Ibid., pp. 539, 553.

23 Materialy XX1V s'yezda KPSS, p. 179.

24 Pravda, 25 October, 1969.

25 The census data for 1897, 1926, 1939 and 1959 are all taken from Strana Sovetov za 50 let, p. 272.

Chapter 3 Socially-Useful Work as a Social Orientation

1 L.I. Brezhnev, "Ocherednye zadachi partii v oblasti sel'skovo khozyaistva," *Kommunist*, 1970, No. 10, p. 29.

2 The table is compiled from data in *Strana Sovetov za 50 let*, p. 165; *Narodnoye khozyaistvo SSSR v 1970 godu*, p. 412.

3 *Altaiskaya pravda*, 8 December, 1970.

4 *Narodnoye khozyaistvo SSSR v 1970 godu*, pp. 277, 283.

5 See *Materialy XXlV s'yezda KPSS*, p. 262.

6 *Ibid*., p. 49.

7 V.I. Lenin, *Collected Works* (Russian), Vol. 35, p. 195.

8 See *Kommunist*, 1971, No. 14, p. 13.

9 See *Sotsialisticheskoye sorevnovanie v SSSR. 1918-1964 gg. Dokumenty i materialy profsoyuzov*, Moscow, 1965, p. 166.

Chapter 4 Social and Political Activity

1 V.G. Mordkovich, "Razvitie obschestvenno-politicheskoi oktivnosti trudyashchikhsya," in *Dukhovnoye razvitie lichnosti*, Sverdlovsk, 1967, pp. 174-175.

2 See L.I. Brezhnev, *Rech' na Vsesoyuznom slyote studentov, 19 October, 1971*, Moscow, 1971, pp. 13-14.

3 The Sociological Research Laboratory of Moscow University has been studying factors in the promotion of the labour and social activity of workers on the *Komsomolets* Collective Farm since 1966.

4 *Materialy XXlV s'yezda KPSS*, p. 82.

Chapter 5 Moral Outlook of Rural Youth

1 *Materialy XVl s'yezda VLKSM*, p. 19

2 See A.G. Zdravomyslov, V.A. Yadov, "Otnoshenie k trudu i tsennostnye orientatsii lichnosti," in *Sotsiologiya v SSSR*, Moscow, 1965; M.N. Rutkevich, "Obshchestvennye potrebnosti sistema obrazovaniya i plany molodovo pokoleniya," *Ural*, 1966, No. 8; V.N. Shubkin, '*Molodyozh' vstupaet v zhizn*', '*Voprosy filosofii*, 1965, No. 5.

3 Sel'skaya molodyozh', Moscow, 1970, pp. 119-120.

4 See Chelovek i yeyo rabota, Moscow, 1967; Molodyozh'. Trud. Uchoba. Dosug, Sverdlovsk, 1969; Molodyozh' i trud, Moscow, 1970; Molodyozh', yeyo interesy, stremleniya, idealy, Moscow, 1969; Sel'skaya molodyozh', Moscow, 1970.

5 Torzhestvo Leninskovo kooperativnovo plana, p. 55.

Chapter 6 Leisure Activities

1 From an unpublished manuscript. Bol'shevik, 1939, No. 11-12, p. 65.

2 See S.G. Strumilin, "Godovoi byudzhet krest'yanina," Vremya, 1923, No. 2; S.G. Strumilin, Byudzhet vremeni russkovo rabochevo i krest'yanina v 1922-1923. Statistiko-eknonmichesky ocherk, Moscow-Leningrad, 1924.

3 V.I. Bolgov, "Kategoriya vremeni v sotsial'nom izmerenii i planirovanii i problema ekonomiki vremeni," Problema byudzheta vremeni trudyashchikhsya, Moscow, 1970, vyp. 6, p. 42.

4 Narodnoye khozyaistvo SSSR v 1970 godu, p. 663.

5 Ibid., p. 670.

6 Ibid., p. 663.

7 L.I. Brezhnev, Leninskim kursom, Vol. 2, p. 87.

8 L.I. Brezhnev, "Ocherednye zadachi partii v oblasti sel'skovo khozyaistva," Kommunist, 1970, No. 10, p. 12.

9 See V.P. Korchagin, L.S. Styrova, Sfera uslug i zanyatnost' naseleniya, Moscow, 1970, p. 85.

10 V.G. Baikova, A.S. Duchal, A.A. Zemtsov, Svobodnoye vremya i vsestoronneye razvitie lichnosti, Moscow, 1965, p. 223.

11 N. Ryabov, "Ispol'zovanie svobodnovo vremeni sel'skoi molodyozhi," Molodyozh' i sotsializm, Moscow, 1967, p. 24. See also V.I. Bolgov, V.P. Smolentsev, "Byudzhety vremeni chlenov semyei kolkhoznikov (po materialam vyborochnykh obsledovanii v Mariiskoi ASSR v 1965-1966 gg.)," Sotsial'nye issledovaniya, Moscow, 1970, vyp. 6, pp. 163-186.

12 See Materialy XVl s'yezda VLKSM, p. 81.

13 Details of changes in the spiritual interests and requirements of rural residents are given in works by I.T. Levykin, *Nekotorye metodologicheskie problemy izucheniya psikhologii krest'yanstva*, Oryol, 1970; Yu.V. Arutyunyan, "Sotsial'nye aspekty kul'turnovo rosta sel'skovo naseleniya," *Voprosy filosofii*, 1968, No. 9, pp. 119-131.

14 See V.G. Baikova, A.S. Duchal, A.A. Zemtsov, *Svobodnoye vremya i vsestoronneye razvitie lichnosti*.

BIBLIOGRAPHY

Soviet literature on rural sociology published since 1960

Anokhina, L.A., Shmeleva, M.N., Kul'tura i byt kolkhoznikov Kalininskoi oblasti, Moscow, 1964.

Arutyunyan, Yu.V., Mekhanizatory sel'skovo khozyaistva SSSR, Moscow, 1960.

Arutyunyan, Yu.V., Vozniknovenie i razvitie massovykh industrial'nykh-kadrov sel'skovo khozyaistva SSSR, Moscow, 1963.

Arutyunyan, Yu.V., Sovetskoye krest'yanstvo v gody velikoi otechestvennoi voiny, Moscow, 1963.

Arutyunyan, Yu.V., Opyt sotsiologicheskovo izucheniya sela, Moscow, 1968.

Arutyunyan, Yu.V., Sotsial'naya struktura sel'skovo naseleniya, Moscow, 1971.

Baranov, M.M., Novye progressivnye formy oplaty truda v kolkhozakh, Moscow, 1967.

Belyanov, V.A., Lichnoye podsobnoye khozyaistvo pri sotsializme, Moscow, 1970.

Bolgov, V.I. (ed.), Sotsial'nye issledovaniya: problemy byudzheta vremeni trudyashchikhsya, Vyp. 6, Moscow, 1970.

Brysyakin, S.K. et al. (eds.), Stanovlenie i razvitie kolkhoznovo stroya v Moldavskoi SSR, Kishinyov, 1971.

Churakov, V.Ya., Suvorova, L.I., Ispol'zovanie trudovykh resursov v kolkhozakh i sovkhozakh, Moscow, 1967.

Davidyuk, G.P. (ed.), Nauchno-tekhnichesky progress i sotsial'nye izmeneniya na sele, Minsk, 1972.

Dobrynina, V.I. (ed.), Molodyozh i trud, Moscown, 1970.

Emel'yanov, A.M. (ed.), Ekonomicheskie i sotsial'nye problemy industrializatsii sel'skovo khozyaistva, Moscow, 1971.

Fishevsky, Yu.K., Ekonomicheskie i sotsial'nye problemy razvitiya sel'skovo khozyaistva SSSR, Moscow, 1969.

Golikov, V.A. (ed.), Sel'skoye khozyaistvo SSSR na sovremennom etape: dostizheniya i perspektivy, Moscow, 1972.

Grigoriev, V.K., Kolkhoznoye pravo, Moscow, 1970.

Grigorovsky, V.E., Alekseyev, M.A., Lichnoye podsobnoye khozyaistvo, Leningrad, 1968.

Gusev, V.V., Kolkhoz kak samoupravlyayemaya sotsial'naya sistema, Moscow, 1971.

Kaminsky, A.E. et al., Razmeshchenie i spetsializatsiya sel'skovo khozyaistvo SSSR, Moscow, 1969.

Kandrenkov, A.A., Kaluzhskaya derevnya, Moscow, 1970.

Karnaukhov, E.S., Lozlov, M.I., Puti povysheniya proizvoditel'nosti truda v sel'skom khozyaistve, Moscow, 1964.

Kolbanovsky, V.N. (ed.), Kollektiv kolkhozov: sotsial'no-psikhologicheskoye issledovanie, Moscow, 1970.

Konstantinov, F.V. (ed.), Stroitel'stvo kommunizma i razvitie obshchestvennykh otnosheniy, Moscow, 1966.

Kuzmin, E.S., Osnovy sotsial'noi psikhologii, Leningrad, 1967.

Laptiev, I.D., Nakoplenie i potreblenie v kolkhozakh, Moscow, 1967.

Lebedev, V.I., Znamenostsy vedut vperyod, Saratov, 1965.

Levykin, I., Nekotorye metodologicheskie problemy izucheniya psikhologii krest'yanstva, Oryol, 1970.

Makovetsky, I.V., Maslova, G.S. (eds.), Byt i iskusstvo russkovo naseleniya Vostochnoi Sibiri, Novosibirsk, 1971.

Medvedev, N.A., "Sotsial'noye planirovanie na sele kak faktor pod'yoma sel'skovo khozyaistvennovo proizvodstva," in Polozov, V.R., Kuzmin, E.S., Chelovek i obshchestvo, Leningrad, 1972.

Monich, Z.I., Intelligentsia v strukture sel'skovo naseleniya (na materialakh Belerusskoi SSR), Minsk, 1971.

Morozov, D.A., Trudoden', den'gi i torgovlya na sele, Moscow, 1965.

Osipov, G.V. (ed.), Sotsiologiya v SSSR, Moscow, 1966.

Osipov, G.V., Szczepanski, J. (eds.), Sotsial'nye problemy truda i proizvodstva, Moscow/Warsaw, 1969.

Ostrovsky, V.B., Kolkhoznoye krest'yanstvo SSSR, Saratov, 1967.

Overchuk, L., "Valovoi dokhod i oplata truda v kolkhozakh," Ekonomika Sovetskoi Ukrainy, 1973, No. 6.

Patrushev, V.D. (ed.), Opyt ekonomiko-sotsiologicheskikh issledovanii v Sibiri, Novosibirsk, 1966.

Perevedentsev, V.P., Zakonomernosti perekhoda ot sotsializma k kommunizmu, Moscow, 1961.

Perevedentsev, V.P., Migratsiya naseleniya i trudsvye problemy Sibiri, Novosibirsk, 1966.

Petrosyan, G.S., Vnerabocheye vremya trudyashchikhsya v SSSR, Moscow, 1965.

Petrov, V.V., Primerny ustav i problemy sotsialisticheskoi zakonnosti v kolkhozakh, Kazan', 1971.

Ryvkina, R.V. (ed.), Sotsiologicheskie issledovaniya, Novosibirsk, 1967.

Sdobnov, S.N., Dve formy sotsialisticheskoi sobstvennosti i puti ikh sblizheniya, Moscow, 1961.

Semin, S.I., Nedelimye fondy i puti sblizheniya kolkhozno-kooperativnoi sobstvennosti s obshchenarodnoi, Moscow, 1961.

Semin, S.I., Preodelenie sotsial'no-ekonomicheskikh razlichiy mezhdu gorodom i derevnei, Moscow, 1973.

Shaibekov, K.A., Pravovye formy oplaty truda v kolkhozakh, Moscow, 1963.

Shcherbina, I.L. (ed.), Kollektiv kolkhoznikov, Moscow, 1970.

Shkurko, V.N., Problemy formirovaniya vsestoronnei razvitoi lichnosti kolkhoznika, Minsk, 1971.

Shmelev, G.A., Lichnoye podsobnoye khozyaistvo i yevo svyazi s obshchestvennym proizvodstvom, Moscow, 1971.

Shubkin, V.N., Sotsiologicheskie opyty, Moscow, 1970 (esp. Chap. 2).

Sidorova, M.I., Obshchestvennye fondy potrebleniya i dokhody kolkhoznikov, Moscow, 1969.

Smirnov, V., "Dvizhenie i ispol'zovanie trudovykh resursov sela," Ekonomicheskie nauki, 1969, No. 5.

Sokhan', L.V., Sotsiologiya na Ukraine, Kiev, 1968.

Staroverov, V.I., Gorod ili derevnya, Moscow, 1972.

Stepanyan, Ts.A., Semyonov, V.S. et al. (eds.), Klassy, sotsial'nye sloi i gruppy v SSSR, Moscow, 1968.

Stepanyan, Ts.A., Semyonov, V.S. et al. (eds.), Problemy izmeneniya sotsial'noi struktury sovetskovo obshchestva, Moscow, 1968.

Teryayeva, A., "Zonal'nye problemy vosproizvodstva rabochei sily i oplata truda v sel'skom khozyaistve," Voprosy ekonomiki, 1968x, No. 1 (see also article by Teryayeva in Voprosy ekonomiki, 1972, No. 5).

Tulepbayev, B.A., Torzhestvo Leninskikh idei sotsialisticheskovo preobrazovaniya sel'skovo khozyaistva v Srednei Azii i Kazakhstana, Moscow, 1971.

Volkov, I.M. (ed.), Razvitie sel'skovo khozyaistva SSSR v poslevoyennye gody (1946-70), Moscow, 1972.

Volovik, L.A. (ed.), Sotsiologiya i ideologiya, Moscow, 1969.

Vlasov, N.S. (eds.), Organizatsiya priozvodstva v sovkhozakh i kolkhozakh, Moscow, 1971.

Yakimov, V.N., Problemy trudovykh resursov v kolkhozakh, Moscow, 1969.

Zabelin, N., Sundetov, S., Ispol'zovanie trudovykh resursov v voprosakh balansa truda, Alma Ata. 1966.

Zaslavskaya, T.I., Raspredelenie po trudu v kolkhozakh, Moscow, 1966.

Zaslavskaya, T.I., Ladenkov, V.N., "Sotsial'no-ekonomicheskie usloviya sozdaniya postoyannykh kedrov v sel'skom khozyaistve Sibiri," Izvestiya Sibirskovo otdeleniya AN SSSR, seriya obshchestvennykh nauk, 1967, No. 11.

Zaslavskaya, T.I., (ed.), Migratsiya sel'skovo naseleniya, Moscow, 1970.

Zdravomyslov, A.G., Yadov, V.A., Trud i razvitie lichnosti, Leningrad, 1965.

Zdravomyslov, A.G., Yadov, V.A., Rozhin, V.P., Chelovek i yevo rabota, Moscow, 1967.

Zinchenko, G.I., Minin, M.K., Ekonomicheskoye stimulirovanie i nauchnaya organizatsiya sel'skovo khozyaistvennovo truda, Moscow, 1968.